ONE
DAY
AT
A
TIME

My journey through leukemia and a stem cell transplant

Marge Johnson

◆ FriesenPress

Suite 300 - 990 Fort St
Victoria, BC, V8V 3K2
Canada

www.friesenpress.com

Copyright © 2017 by Marge Johnson
First Edition — 2017

All rights reserved.

No part of this publication may be reproduced in any form, or by any means, electronic or mechanical, including photocopying, recording, or any information browsing, storage, or retrieval system, without permission in writing from FriesenPress.

ISBN
978-1-4602-9458-1 (Hardcover)
978-1-4602-9459-8 (Paperback)
978-1-4602-9460-4 (eBook)

1. BIOGRAPHY & AUTOBIOGRAPHY, MEDICAL

Distributed to the trade by The Ingram Book Company

Therefore do not worry about tomorrow, for tomorrow will worry about itself. Each day has enough trouble of its own.
(Matthew 6:34, NIV)

Stacey,
It is so nice to meet you... happy reading!
Marge Ihm

The cover design is a blood smear magnification showing chronic lymphocytic leukemia (CLL) cells.

Dedication

After completing my story, I recognized a series of events had taken place in bringing my project into being. It all started with my broken hip. Instead of filling each day with an endless list of tasks, (giving me much satisfaction when crossed off), I was forced to sit and rest, my busy day always shortened by physical fatigue and pain, especially in my leg on my injured hip side.

This resulted in me experiencing long evenings of mental boredom. I considered many "resting" activities, but none satisfied. Then a simple suggestion to solve my boredom issue, "If you write your story, (of leukemia), I'll read it…!" became my initial inspiration!

As I began writing my story, I couldn't help but be reminded of the incredible support of love, care, acts of kindness, and finances that were offered. I looked forward to evenings, my time to scribe, inspired and motivated by the continuous reminder of ways I was supported. I continued my story to fruition, motivated to pay forward, (or back), in story form, to those who walked this journey with me. To all of you who gave of yourself to me in large or small ways, whether mentioned in my story or not; I dedicate this book.

Acknowledgements

Thank you my son, Jay, for your willingness to spontaneously drop by to assist me with the computer skills required in sending my manuscript and necessary documents to my publisher.

Thank you my friend, Deb, for sharing in my excitement as I wrote my story and for carefully reading through my manuscript to offer helpful editing feedback.

Thank you Uncle Walter for your few, yet wise words regarding the completion of my story, "Good things take time." I continually reminded myself of those four words. They prevented me from rushing through… The gift of time to complete my story the best I could was always on my side.

CONTENTS

1	Going Home	11
2	Renovations	13
3	Graft Versus Host Disease	15
4	Back to Vancouver	17
5	Memories of Not Long Ago	21
6	Another Hickman Line	36
7	A New Room and Good Shit	39
8	More Hospital Days	41
9	The ATG Plan, Prednisone, And Real Food	45
10	Visitors and Day Passes	50
11	To Grandma's House with Laura	53
12	No Longer Living	62
13	Back to Grandma's House with Joy	80
14	The Wedding Dress	83
15	More Needles and a Very Bloody Nose	85
16	Medication Side Effects	91
17	At Grandma's House with Neenee	96
18	Very Bad Bleeding	99
19	A New Complication	106
20	Back to Grandma's House	111
21	Jean C. Barber Lodge	117
22	Going Home Again	125

GOING HOME

"I'M DRIVING!" I ANNOUNCED AS I grabbed the keys, jiggling them off the ends of my fingers. I skipped down the steps from Grandma's house and headed to our Subaru parked in front of the house along the curb of Thirtieth Avenue. I couldn't keep the happy expression off my face.

"Are you sure you're up to it?" my husband Al asked, sharing my excitement. "Let me know as soon as you feel tired and I'll take over."

"I will," I promised.

I was finally on my way home, for real. My bone marrow transplant in October was now behind me. I waited patiently and anxiously until I heard the words that I was waiting for from my hematologist Doctor Smith.

"You can go home for Christmas!"

Then he became very serious so the rest of his message would be heard loud and clear. "If you have any diarrhea, headaches, nausea, vomiting or a fever, or don't feel quite right at any time while you are home, you will need to get back to the hospital here immediately. After Christmas, we will need to see you every week here in Vancouver for a while."

I had developed a sense of security while being monitored so closely in Vancouver and now it felt like I was leaving that security behind. Doctor Smith reminded me of how vulnerable my body was. Even though my health seemed stable, my condition could change rapidly. That's why his permission for me to go home meant he had confidence that I would be OK; that was important to me.

Being able to go home to my family after spending three months in Vancouver meant everything to me. I kept saying over and over, "I feel like I've won a million dollars!"

"Woohoo! Only 274 kilometers to Hope!" I called out, reading the first highway sign, and smiling from ear to ear over at Al. It was hard to contain my excitement. I kept repeating to myself, "I'm actually on my way home...!" It was the first of many highway signs that I woohooed at as we merged onto the freeway from Grandview Highway. I hadn't been outside of Vancouver since being admitted into Vancouver General Hospital in September.

It seemed like just moments later we pulled over for a snack and bathroom break in Princeton.

"I'll drive from here," my husband offered.

"That's OK. I'm feeling great and I want to keep driving."

Al didn't protest. He had spent the last three months driving back and forth every weekend to see me. The passenger seat suited him just as fine as the driver's seat suited me.

It seemed like the easiest and fastest drive home ever.

RENOVATIONS

IT WAS GOOD TO BE home; the best Christmas present ever! And as I took a quick tour of my house, I noticed an extra bonus; my house was spic and span, all ready for Christmas!

But after the holidays everyone went back to their own routines and responsibilities. Where did that leave me? I felt well and had lots of energy, but was not able to return to work. Doctor Smith reminded me that I needed to stay close to home and give myself lots of time to recover.

Delving into my husband's company's bookkeeping that I had fallen behind with while in Vancouver would be the first stay-at-home project I could take on. The end of January seemed like a reasonable deadline for me to be caught up. I paced myself accordingly; I looked forward to a new project developing in my mind after the book work was caught up.

During my stay in Vancouver for almost three months post-transplant, I found myself watching renovation shows on TV; and thoroughly enjoying them. Now being home, all day and every day, I realized how run-down our house had become. After all, three rambunctious boys and a girl tearing around the house for years took its toll on the place. The renovated houses that were shown on TV looked fantastic. They inspired and motivated me to start working on our place. My husband Al came on board too. Since I wasn't able to go back to work for a while, it seemed like the perfect project for me to take on. I planned to be back teaching in the fall, so this would give me a good window of time to get some renovations done.

I planned out the projects, and Al and I worked hard to see things come together. We started by pulling off the old baseboards, and door and window trims. Al refinished the hardwood floors while I picked out the paint colors for the three bedrooms and painted them. I also bought and painted new baseboards and trim to replace the old. Al carefully measured, cut, and installed them into the newly painted bedrooms.

Wow! It was starting to look just as good as the finished renovations I watched on T.V! With all our kids gone from home except Zach, we had lots of room to work. I could go at my own speed as I didn't have other responsibilities to juggle outside the home. If something didn't get done, it could always wait until tomorrow.

I was excited about the renovation results and they motivated me to keep going. We accomplished so much in just two months!

It sure was nice being at home; recovering! Haha! I didn't feel much different than before my transplant. I guess I was just one of those people who sailed through it.

GRAFT VERSUS HOST DISEASE

"IT'S PROBABLY THE FLU. THERE is a lot of that going around. But if you think you've lost a lot of fluid through vomiting and diarrhea, go to Emergency and they will give you an IV bag to rehydrate you. Try not to vomit, stay away from milk products, and you should start to feel better," was my family doctor's advice over the phone.

So that's what I did. I went to the hospital to get rehydrated, in fact twice in four days. Each time they sent me home after receiving a bag of saline solution, and each time I felt worse, much worse. My diarrhea looked like dark, green, watery fluid, the color of an avocado peel. And it was pouring out of me like a tap on full blast.

"I'm calling Doctor Smith," I told Al; and left a message for Doctor Smith to return my call.

Shortly after, "Al!" I called from my bed, using all the energy I had to project my voice to reach him. "Carry me to the bathroom. I can't get up. I have to go right away! Hurry, or I won't make it!"

My limp body dangled from Al's arms as he carried me to the bathroom. I was so confused. What was happening to me? I couldn't even get myself to the bathroom. By the hour, feeling weaker and weaker, my physical condition was rapidly declining. I had never felt this exhausted and weak ever before in my life.

"Call an ambulance Al," my voice tired and strained. "I can't sit and wait in Emergency again. I don't have the strength."

As I sat on the toilet spewing out liters of this strange colored, watery fluid, Doctor Smith returned my call. My quiet voice, almost a whisper now, explained what was happening to me. I turned the phone onto speaker so Al could hear our conversation.

Doctor Smith knew right away. "You sound very weak and what you are describing to me tells me you are very sick, Marge. You have Graft Versus Host Disease, (GVHD), of the gut and need to get to the hospital right away."

Of course! All of a sudden it made complete sense to me. That's exactly what it was. The instant diagnosis gave me a moment of relief; quickly interrupted by the arrival of two paramedics in the bathroom doorway asking me for the details of my condition.

In simple terms Graft Versus Host Disease is a battle that takes place between the transplanted stem cells, (my brother's; which is the graft), and the patient's body, (me, the host). This can happen when the new stem cells reject and attack the recipient's body.

"Don't let them send you home this time!" my sister, Joy, called out from my kitchen window as I was carried out on a stretcher to the ambulance.

That's exactly what I told the doctor in Emergency when she was ready to discharge me for the third time after I had been rehydrated again.

With all the energy I had, "I'm not going home! I'm staying because I have GVHD," I rebutted.

There were no beds available so I stayed on the stretcher for the night. I don't remember much except that I was woken up in the night as an elderly lady lying next to me got up and grabbed the pillow from under my head as I slept.

"What was that?" I looked up to see the little, old lady head back to her bed carrying my pillow! "Nurse, nurse..." as one walked past. "Could you give me my pillow back? The lady lying over there with three pillows pulled mine from under my head..."

Emergency was bustling. But when I was eventually transferred to a bed with a commode next to me and a curtain all around, I began to settle in.

BACK TO VANCOUVER

AFTER THREE DAYS I WAS moved from the emergency area to a room with two other patients. I tried to greet the patient next to me once; hoping to add interest to our day, but she couldn't hear me. My frail voice didn't carry. Oh well; I realized I didn't have any energy to visit or care anyways.

I experienced extreme, abdominal pain. I've never been one to seek pain medication, but I soon realized how important it was. I learned to manage my pain by staying on top of it, instead of chasing it. As soon as I felt the pain returning, I would press my call button, anxiously struggling for and anticipating pain relief. I was given mostly morphine, administered through a needle the nurse would poke into my stomach, and the occasional Tylenol. With more pain relief, my days became much less stressful and my ability to cope both emotionally and physically increased significantly.

For the next ten days, every day became the same: eat, race to the bathroom, back to bed, pain medication, and exhaustion. Most of my day was spent lying on my back, completely fatigued, and perking up for a bit when company came to my bedside. They would have to come close to hear me; my voice a quiet strained whisper. I would press the button on the side railing of my bed to raise the top half of my bed so I could sit up slightly for visiting. (I was too weak to pull myself into a sitting position on my own.) My daughter described me as being one with the mattress.

The nights were quiet and peaceful, despite being in a hospital and sharing a room with two others. The only sound I woke to and enjoyed was an owl hooting outside my window.

No matter what I ate, no matter what medication I was given, the continuous IV bag that I was hooked up to could not keep up to the amount of fluid I was losing.

Because my doctor was leaving on a family vacation during spring break shortly after I was admitted into the hospital, I had several different doctors overseeing my care.

I wondered, "Does anyone notice the color of, or how much diarrhea I have compared to the amount of fluid I'm taking in?" (A chart was taped on the bathroom door for me to fill out to keep track of the volume I was losing.) "This isn't your everyday diarrhea!"

It seemed no one was alarmed by my symptoms or my continuous lack of improvement. Every morning a doctor would pay me a visit: check my heart rate and lungs, ask about my pain level, and then continue on his merry way.

I remember a doctor once saying to me, "If you're not improving, you're getting worse. Your body can only continue for so long without improvement." I now realized the truth of that and believed it described me precisely. It made me feel serious concern and urgency about my condition.

"Are the doctors conversing with my hematologist in Vancouver?" I asked a nurse tending to me one day.

"I'm sure the doctor has everything under control," she replied quickly, nervously, matter of fact, not assuring me at all. She was young, maybe new at her profession, possibly intimidated by my concern, and I wondered if she was afraid to bother the doctor about it.

"Could you please ask the doctor and let me know as soon as you can? I need to know." I didn't want to be rude but I needed assurance and her reply hadn't satisfied me.

Well the nurse didn't ask the doctor my question. She said he was very busy and wasn't sure where he was. I felt her lack of effort on my behalf wasn't acceptable and decided I couldn't let it go. My condition was too serious for me to be left wondering. I made a call to Doctor Smith's office using the Vancouver contacts that I had kept on my cell. I left a message and my call was returned shortly.

"Hi, yes it's Marge..."

It was easy to describe my condition when he asked me as I lay exhausted and weak, flat on my bed. I explained how I wasn't getting better and reminded him of my continued full-on, strange colored diarrhea.

"Yes, I will get someone to my phone," I continued.

I pressed my call bell. When my nurse entered the room, I was sitting up already and forcefully extended my arm towards her with my phone. "Here, it's for you!"

Confused, she hesitantly took my cell phone. "Hello?..." and with it, left the room.

I was relieved. I had taken the necessary plan of action; contacting Doctor Smith. With an exhausted sigh, I lay back again on my bed and then, wondered if I would get my phone back.

Later that day I was told that I would be going to Vancouver General Hospital as soon as a medical flight was available, but they could not give me any idea as to when that might be. "Hopefully in the next day or two..."

While my daughter was visiting me the next morning, my nurse came in. "A plane has arrived at the airport for you. You will be leaving for Vancouver as soon as the paramedics arrive. There is space for one other passenger..."

My eyes immediately glanced over at my daughter, "Well that's you, Carolyn! Dad can't leave work, so run home, get packed up, and be back ASAP. You're flying to Vancouver with me!"

I had not wanted to go back there. I had only been home less than three months and had been enjoying every bit of it. I had never thought I would be heading back to Vancouver, especially in this condition. But by now I realized my desperate situation and knew that if I was going to get better, it meant being where the specialists were that I so badly needed.

It was my first Easter ever, spent in the hospital; Easter Monday I was flown out of Penticton.

I had the best spot on the plane. As they placed me on my stretcher inside, my face was right up against a window for a view that I enjoyed all the way to Vancouver.

I also noticed the pilot; tall, young, and handsome, very professional looking in his uniform, as he efficiently carried on with his tasks. "I need to get his phone number...," I thought spontaneously,

"...to give to my daughter!" Unfortunately I was too weak to carry through with the idea. A missed opportunity, I figured!

MEMORIES OF NOT LONG AGO

AS I LAY IN BED, in the same ward I had my transplant six months past, it brought back a flood of memories.

It all started when I decided to have a varicose vein surgically removed from my leg. In the process, the surgeon found an enlarged lymph node. Feeling perplexed and uncertain about it, he removed the lymph node and had it sent to Vancouver for further testing. The results were cancerous. And so the journey began...

My first appointment was with my family doctor. She told me about the cancerous lymph node and that I would be seeing an oncologist in Kelowna to discuss it further. She suggested I take someone with me so Al came along. My appointment was at 9:00 a.m. in the Cancer Clinic, part of Kelowna General Hospital (KGH).

As we walked through the front entrance, it felt surreal, in a dismal way. I noticed patients of all ages wandering through the receptionist area; some in hospital gowns, some in street clothing, many with no hair, some wearing head coverings of different sorts...

We sat in the waiting area, a coffee table in front of us, with scattered jigsaw pieces, and the puzzle box standing to show the finished result. I hoped to find a few pieces, but were too soon escorted to a small doctor's office where we sat some more, door closed, waiting quietly; Al more nervous than myself. A medical person entered with a clip board, introduced herself, asked a list of standard medical questions, recorded my responses on her clip board, and then left. We waited...another medical person entered the room with a clip board, introduced himself..., and left the room.

"Why is this taking so long?" I asked Al. "It's almost noon and I still don't know anything...why don't they just tell me what's wrong? It seems like they're trying to avoid telling me!"

I imagined the medical staff arguing outside the closed door.

"You tell her!"

"No, you tell her!"

"I'm not telling her!"

Finally, my recently assigned oncologist walked in and sat down...

It wasn't good news, especially the way she told it. In short, she said, "You have Chronic Lymphocytic Leukemia, (CLL), a type of blood cancer. Because it's in your blood; flowing through your body, we have no way of targeting it like, say, breast cancer. There is no cure for it."

"Is there something we can do?" Al asked, offering diet or other life style suggestions, hoping...

"No, there is nothing that can be done about it. You will just have to live with the fact. Some people live longer than others..."

That was the abrupt end to my appointment. No smiles, no encouragement, and no hope from my oncologist.

Al did not like her at all! I couldn't blame him. It took over three hours of waiting and wondering before she dropped the bomb and then left us feeling helpless and hopeless.

"There is some good news though," I offered on the drive home. "I won't have to go through terrible bouts of chemotherapy. Those drugs are brutal...

"Your grandpa had leukemia; he died when he was old." I reminded Al.

I couldn't believe I had cancer. I didn't feel or see any symptoms that would convince me to believe otherwise.

I decided not to think much more about my diagnosis. I felt healthy and strong and since there was "nothing that could be done about it", I put the subject on the back burner. For the most part, I continued to live as before hearing about my diagnosis.

Al didn't fare with the news as well as I did, so I challenged him; hoping to put his mind at ease. "You never know, you could have leukemia too, maybe it just hasn't been discovered yet...or you could die in a car accident tomorrow, and be dead before me."

I did enjoy the temporary change in Al's behavior though! "Here, let me get that...I'll do it for you...you have to take it easy, you're sick you know..." He even offered, "I'll mow the lawn!"

Shortly after my diagnosis a bone marrow biopsy was requested by my oncologist. It would serve as a base line from when I was first diagnosed so the progression of my leukemia could be observed and monitored.

I was getting used to a regular routine of walking back and forth to and from the hospital, only five blocks from my house, and enjoyed the exercise and fresh air it offered. However, instead of providing my usual blood samples, today I walked to the hospital for my scheduled biopsy appointment.

"You look like you're in good spirits, Marge," the doctor observed as he met me in the waiting area. It was unusual for him to see such a pleasant, relaxed countenance on someone just prior to receiving this type of procedure.

"Are you nervous at all?" he probed.

"Not really," I responded.

"Are you familiar with a bone marrow biopsy?" he asked, continuing to probe.

"Not really," I repeated, starting to feel a bit nervous.

"Well...it's not the most comfortable procedure..."

I followed him into a small, narrow room, not much bigger than an average bedroom closet; in it, a narrow bed. He handed me a folded hospital gown to change into and left the room.

Moments later he returned with another medical person who introduced himself. It started to feel crowded...

"...I'm here to support and coach you..." was all he said.

And the doctor explained to me, "I'm going to start with some local anesthetic to freeze the area...a little sting..."

"You mean a big sting!" I felt, and said to myself.

I was left alone for a few minutes while the anesthetic did its job, now regretting not having done some prior research...

When they returned, the first doctor explained the procedure. "I will use a needle to extract a small sample of bone marrow from your pelvis...since the inside of your bone cannot be numbed, you may feel some pressure, discomfort, dull pain..."

I felt every bit of the pain he described times 1000! This was the first time I had been in any kind of discomfort due to my illness.

Because of my continued healthy wellbeing, I had been in denial of the seriousness of my leukemia. But now this simple but painful procedure traumatized me and gave me the wakeup call I wasn't sure I wanted to deal with.

I left the room with a sore behind, feeling humiliated and embarrassed, and teary eyed; like a little girl coming out from her room after being disciplined with a big spanking. I had not prepared myself in any way of what a bone marrow biopsy entailed.

I didn't feel able to walk home and now regretted not bringing my phone. I'd have to face the receptionist...

"Can I use the phone?" I asked her, my mouth quivering and eyes tearing.

"Hi Al...I need a ride home please," I whimpered.

That was the first of four bone marrow biopsies. My neighbor Karen, a lab technician, happened to be coaching me during one of my biopsies. The doctor left the room while I was asked to stay a few minutes to be monitored before leaving. Karen showed me the vile that contained the piece of bone he extracted from me. It looked like a broken piece of tooth.

Apart from my hospital walks and appointments, life continued as usual. I concluded I would die from leukemia at a ripe, old age, like many do.

So did my ear specialist. After looking at my file, he responded with, "Oh, you've got leukemia...," and casually added, "That's OK, you'll probably live till you're eighty or ninety anyways." I agreed and appreciated his blessed words on my life!

While another doctor, during an appointment, couldn't get past my diagnosis. "Oh! That's terrible! When did you find that out?" He continued on and on about it.

I had to remind him, "My appointment isn't about my leukemia..."

But then, about five years later, my leukemia suddenly took a turn for the worse. My blood counts, that had been closely monitored, (and normal), since my diagnosis, were changing rapidly.

A stem cell transplant was strongly suggested by my recently assigned hematologist, Doctor Smith. "The optimum time for you to have a transplant is now, while you are still young, strong, and healthy enough to handle the procedure and its risky side effects. It will take some time as we begin the process of finding the best donor match for you..."

My next appointment with Doctor Smith was in Kelowna. He flew once every few months from Vancouver for prearranged appointments. This time I brought my friend, Noree, and a piece of paper, as both were suggested.

Doctor Smith explained in great detail the process, risks, financial costs, pros, cons, success statistics; the works...of a stem cell transplant. In the middle of it all, I had questions.

"Ask me at the end of my explanation," he said each time I attempted to interrupt; I didn't want to forget my questions.

And every once in a while, he would interrupt his own spiel and say, "This is a very important decision you are going to make."

As he continued, he kept eye contact with me as if trying to read my thoughts. Occasionally he would interrupt himself again to remind and impress on me, "This is a very serious matter."

He presented a well prepared speech; the information very thorough, clear and concise. By the time he was finished, (he talked non-stop for about 45 minutes), my questions had all been answered. All I was left with was a very overwhelming feeling from all the information passed on to me. I was glad Noree accompanied me. She would help me remember the details.

During that time, Al had read about chelation in the local paper, did some research on the internet, and wanted me to have some treatments; anything to help cure me of my leukemia.

Basically, chelation is a medical procedure that removes poisonous metals from the body; the chelating agent is administered intravenously. (It has had many successful results on a variety of serious health issues.)

Doctor Whittle, a medical doctor that was now advocating alternative medicine, had set up a chelation treatment clinic in Penticton. After I had a few treatments, he suggested I have some blood work done to see how I was faring. The morning the results arrived in his office, he called me.

"Hi Marge, it's Doctor Whittle. I received your blood results this morning. I want to talk to you about them. Are you sitting down...?"

He told me that my blood results were very concerning and that conventional medicine would be necessary to deal with my leukemia.

"I strongly suggest you listen to your hematologist and follow the treatment plan he recommends. It might involve chemotherapy and even a bone marrow transplant."

I did not want to hear that news. I thought the chelation was working. I had been having some symptoms of leukemia the last few months, but the chelation seemed to make a difference, especially with my night sweats. I would wake up soaking wet and cold. (Having already experienced a season of hot flashes, I knew these were different.) I started wearing a towel around my neck to wipe me dry. It would happen several times each night. I was not sleeping well because of it. Partly because of the symptom, but then I would stay awake worrying about the progression of my leukemia. The chelation seemed to have put an abrupt stop to that symptom!

But I believed Doctor Whittle knew what he was talking about and had my best interest in mind. He also had leukemia, underwent chemotherapy, and had a bone marrow transplant. He fared just fine through it all. Even in his seventies, he was still going strong.

...phone calls, appointments, e-mails, and more phone calls; constant reminders of my CLL.

All of a sudden it felt like time was racing by. My oldest son Jay and his fiancée Chelsey were getting married in Cancun, Mexico. They had been planning their wedding for almost a year and now the date was less than two months away. Would I be able to go?

I asked Doctor Smith about it. His answer was simple. "If you are feeling well, you can go; if not, you're not going anywhere."

I had been struggling with a cold for most of the winter. I had viruses in my eyes that continually lingered, even though I had seen my family doctor several times and tried numerous medications prescribed. I had changing periodic and peculiar pain areas on my legs accompanied by large swollen lumps, smaller lumps that crowded my hair line in the back of my neck and behind my ears, and the occasional flu symptoms.

"I have to stay well, be careful, and look after myself...I have to go to Mexico. I can't miss my son's wedding!" I kept telling myself.

I took a leave from my part-time catering job; it was starting to take its toll on my body.

As their wedding date crept closer, I quietly struggled until I convinced myself and decided, "If I can't go to their wedding, it's not the end of the world. They'll take lots of pictures and a video for me. It's only a week. I'll get over it." Doctor Smith was leaving the decision to go to Mexico or stay home up to me. I booked our family's flights for Cancun, including mine. I closely monitored my wellbeing. During the week prior to our departure, I still had my eye viruses, and the continued lumps and bumps, but overall, I felt well.

I thoroughly enjoyed the holiday; the wedding, family and friends, delicious prepared meals, and the tropical setting. It was such a wonderful distraction and escape from the world I was struggling with at home. I surprisingly noticed my eyes even cleared up while we were there. (I don't know how or why; was it the water?)

Two days after we returned from Mexico, the phone started ringing again, thrusting me back into my reality.

"We are going to start you on some chemotherapy treatments in preparation for your transplant...in Penticton...oncology department."

I was worried. I had seldom taken medication and the thought of chemotherapy frightened me.

"I'm really stressed, Al. I hate taking drugs. This is starting to scare me. I don't know if I can do this." I said one night, lying next to him.

"What day is it today?" he asked.

"Thursday," I replied, wondering if he was even listening.

"What day do you start chemotherapy?" Maybe he was listening.

"Next Tuesday." I answered.

"Well then, why are you worried today? Tuesday is almost a week away. One day at a time." He casually responded, rolled over, and went to sleep.

"Since when did he get to be so smart?" I wondered to myself. It was exactly what I needed to hear as I too dozed off to sleep.

The next morning I thanked him for his wise words.

"I said that?!" He couldn't recall. That's when I realized where the advice really came from!

9:00 Tuesday morning came sooner than I hoped. The room I entered for my treatment had reclining chairs facing one another like a sitting room. I chose an available chair and a nurse came and explained the process to me. She wanted me to know what I could expect from the day ahead. I was immediately hooked up to an IV which the chemo would be transmitted through.

I was also given Benadryl, in case my body reacted to its first introduction to chemo. And it did; my body's urge to get out of my chair and walk around was the first sign. In the middle of my stroll around the unit, I suddenly felt weak, sick, and couldn't get back to my chair fast enough. A nurse was by my side immediately, adding Benadryl to my IV and slowing down the chemo drip into my body. I started vomiting, shaking, and my feet were kicking out of control as I vibrated in my chair. The nurse quickly drew the curtain around me. (I hadn't noticed the curtain until then and was glad for it.) With patients in other chairs facing me, I needed some privacy; although the sound effects were still loud and clear!

Not long after my flamboyant reaction, my body calmed down and the Benadryl knocked me out. I slept through the rest of the day. When I awoke, it was already late afternoon. The chairs around me were all deserted and one nurse left lingering with me. Immediately aware of my waking, she unhooked my IV.

"You can go home now," she said with a compassionate smile.

My next chemo treatment was four weeks later and started the same way. My body reacted again, but in a much different way.

"The top of my head feels prickly and itchy," I told the nurse. She came over.

And then immediately, "My throat feels like it's closing in. It's getting harder to breathe." She reacted quickly, adding more Benadryl and something else...

A couple of minutes later I commented, "What beautiful Christmas decorations they put up in here!" as I glanced around the room, slurring my words at Carolyn. (She had dropped in to visit.)

Carolyn looked at me, confused, then at the nurse.

The nurse didn't miss a beat; grinning, she responded to Carolyn's bewildered look. "Your mom's fine. I gave her some happy pills!"

I had one more chemo treatment; bringing my blood counts in line for my stem cell transplant that would take place in Vancouver.

In August, a month before I was to move there, I got a phone call from my sister-in-law Violet. She was offering me a place to stay in Vancouver while I recovered.

"You can stay at my mother's place... She will be upstairs. You can share the kitchen, but live downstairs; it has two bedrooms and a bathroom."

At the time, I didn't realize how generous her offer was; for me and many others who would come to help me in the months to come.

When I first arrived on the bone marrow transplant ward at Vancouver General Hospital I was escorted to my room. I noticed a pleasant looking lady sitting in a chair by the window glancing over at me. "Do you mind if I open the curtains?" I bravely asked my new roommate as I entered.

"Not at all!" Velma replied enthusiastically.

The curtains that separated our beds stayed open all day and every day that we spent together in VGH. Although she aged me by twenty years, our friendship grew quickly as we spent twenty-four seven together for those few weeks.

I was on the fifteenth floor of the Jim Pattison Pavilion facing North; the million dollar view that I enjoyed for the three weeks that I was in the hospital. In the distance I could see North and West Van nestled against the Coastal Mountains. Right below my window was the helicopter pad that flew emergency patients to VGH. West Broadway was the main bustling street down below, just beyond the helicopter pad. North of West Broadway was Charleson Park in front view with Grandville Island over to the left. A little farther left was Stanley Park and Burrard Inlet. Every day Velma and I counted the ships that continually came and left the Inlet. Beyond Grandville Island and Charleson Park was False Creek. I watched continuous traffic flow back and forth on the three bridges over False Creek: Burrard, Granville, and Cambie Street Bridge connecting to the beautiful downtown Vancouver. From the fifteenth floor, the three-dimensional view of each unique and detailed high rise building was mesmerizing. All the action inside the window frame was like watching an ever-changing picture.

The scenery was as beautiful at night as it was midday. As the skies grew dark, lights flicked on, appearing as rows and columns of tiny squares outlining the high rise structures. Some lights had special effects, blinking, changing patterns, and colors. I spent many hours day and night, sitting on the arm of my chair with my feet on the seat, right up to the window sill; the perfect height for the best panoramic view.

Thanksgiving weekend was creeping up and I dreaded spending it in the hospital. I remembered all the wonderful turkey dinners my family enjoyed around our big dining room table. We always had extra family join us, usually my parents, and often my brother, James, and his kids from Merritt; the more, the merrier. But this

Thanksgiving it would just be Al and my two youngest kids, Carolyn and Zach, coming for a quick visit.

How would I keep them entertained in my hospital room? After a few hours they'd get bored and want to leave the hospital, especially Zach. I'd be left alone...

I had a great idea! "Could I have a day pass, maybe for just a couple of hours...since it's Thanksgiving weekend...and my family will be here?" I asked the doctor the day before they were to arrive; hoping...

"That won't be possible, Marge. With your transplant in just a few days, we can't risk you getting sick. With all the medication you've been on to prepare you for your transplant, your immune system is compromised. We can't take the chance," was his reply.

I kept thinking about Thanksgiving. I talked to the nurse. She had a better idea. She let me book the staff/conference room for the evening my family arrived. We ordered pizza in, watched Modern Family episodes that Carolyn brought, and played the Wii. My exhausted husband could relax and have a snooze on the couch too. It was a good Thanksgiving after all; one I wouldn't forget.

I only experienced one very sick episode the morning of my transplant. I recall the extremely painful headache; the worst I had ever experienced, and intense vomiting. The nurse told me it was my body's reaction to the accumulation of prescribed medications pumped into my body in preparation of my transplant.

Fortunately my reaction was short-lived and I was able to rest and relax the afternoon of my stem cell transplant. It was scheduled for 5:00 that evening. My brother, Rob, was my donor, a perfect 10/10 match. He had been across the hall that morning where his stem cells had been extracted.

"How did it go? What was it like?" I asked him, thankful it wasn't nearly as invasive or painful as a bone marrow transplant. With new medical technology, marrow was no longer physically extracted from the donor's bone.

"It was amazingly simple; a mere prick in the arm. And I don't feel any different, not even tired. It was just like giving blood."

Rob's blood was extracted through an IV process. It then flowed through an instrument that separated the stem cells, (that

I needed), from the rest of his blood. The stem cells were collected into bags and the remainder of his blood was transmitted back into his body through another IV. Like Rob said, nothing short of amazing!

Two nurses entered my room with two bags of pink colored blood, Rob's stem cells. They double checked my name, birth date, and ID number as well as the numbers on the blood products. (A simple mistake could have devastating consequences.)

One nurse hung the blood products up on my IV pole and connected them to my Hickman line. Rob stayed for a while to watch his stem cells being transmitted into my body. It was exciting and intriguing at first. But after watching the first bag of cells flow into my body, we all lost interest. Rob and one of the nurses left, Velma went back to her side of the room, and I visited with the nurse who stayed through to the end of the three hour procedure. (One nurse needed to stay and monitor my body's response to the new cells.)

Although it was very uneventful, there was a major intruder entering my body.

My condition was stable following my transplant. I would soon be discharged on the condition that I would have someone with me while recovering in case of any emergency.

I hadn't thought of that! "Who could stay with me? Everyone was busy with their own lives and jobs, and I was staying 200 miles from home!"

"What a perfect situation!" my brother, Rob, explained to me. "Anna will be able to look after you. She is an experienced care giver and will be at the house for a few weeks. She will be around in case of any problems. I'm around if you need me too." (My brother, Rob, and his wife Violet both resided in Vancouver.)

Anna is Violet's cousin from Hungary who had come to look after her aunt, (Violet's mom), at her house for a while, to give Violet some respite. But just days before my discharge from VGH, Violet's mother passed away. Now it would be just Anna and me at the house for a few weeks until she returned to Hungary.

I called it Grandma's house in Dunbar Village; a beautiful area in Vancouver and a ten minute drive to the hospital. When I was discharged from the hospital to Grandma's house in mid-October, I used the driving program offered by the Masons for patients in the Vancouver area; the best suited transportation available for my situation. All I had to do was phone them to arrange rides for my appointment times at the hospital. They would pick me up right at my front door, drop me off at the hospital entrance I needed, and then bring me home when I was done. I didn't have a car in Vancouver, as I was advised not to drive post-transplant, (orders from Doctor Smith). The busy transit system wasn't an option either; I was a high risk for catching viruses or bacteria from other transit users because of my weak immune system. By December, I had the strength and enjoyed walking the beautiful, seven kilometer trek.

Grandma's house was an ideal location for me. A strip of amenities on Dunbar Street started less than a block away from where I lived; a perfect walking distance for me. I got myself a library card; the library was two blocks from Grandma's house. I accessed the internet, computers, a few books, and movies. There were coffee shops, a bakery, unique cafes, and restaurants. Stong's Groceries, a produce store, and Shopper's Drug Mart were all within a few blocks of Grandma's house. I depended on and enjoyed those conveniences daily.

Violet picked me up the day I was discharged from VGH. Anna was at Grandma's house to greet me with a warm hug at the door when I arrived.

Anna didn't speak any English, nor did I speak Hungarian, so our communication with each other involved smiling often, drawing pictures, using our hands, and even a bit of acting. Then, when Violet would drop in, she would explain any confusion or questions we had with each other. So it was a quiet atmosphere at Grandma's house until Violet would stop by; then the conversations would buzz back and forth from English to Hungarian.

There were only three days that I was very ill while at Grandma's house and Anna always seemed to be there for me. Even when it meant her getting up in the middle of the night and putting her hand on my back as I was bent over, vomiting. She cooked special food to help soothe my mouth and throat when it became raw and sore. She always let me know that she was there, checking on me every morning and keeping a close eye on me throughout each day, making sure I was OK. I never felt alone. I missed her presence when she left back for Hungary in November.

Although I spent the next seven weeks at Grandma's house on my own, (except for a short-term Australian roommate), the house continued to bustle with family and friends coming to visit and support me. Sometimes it felt like I was running a bed and breakfast as we texted or phoned back and forth making arrangements.

"When are you coming...? I'll need to let Violet know..."

"Great! Those dates will work out well for me..."

And when they arrived, "I'll show you your room. Here are your towels...I'm so glad you came..."

Days like these made me think to myself, "I feel like I'm on a holiday; little responsibility and lots of visiting. Enjoy it while it lasts!"

My hair started falling out a few weeks after my transplant. I was expecting that to happen; a side effect from my medication. I was reminded of our family dog Maggie; continually combing out loose hair. The only difference was Maggie's do looked more beautiful and kempt as it was brushed. My hair do became scruffy looking and thin.

I was having a feeling sorry for myself morning as I headed to the hospital for my regular treatment one day. I particularly noticed how other patients often, and some always, had their spouse or a close family member accompany them during checkups and treatments as out patients, (many moved with them to Vancouver temporarily). I usually went alone and this day I especially felt the loneliness of being away from my family. As I found an available chair for myself I closed the curtain around me which I normally kept open. My hospital day was usually a social time for me, but not today: it was time for a quiet, anticipated cry.

"How come I'm always here by myself? My hair's all falling out. I could use a friend right now," I grumbled in thought to myself, as well as to the Man upstairs. The tears ran down my face. I pulled the garbage can close to my chair so I could comb through my hair with my fingers and drop all the loose hairs into it. It had become my new habit.

Suddenly, my attention turned from self-pity to the voices on the other side of the curtain. They sounded familiar...

Immediately I realized who they were. Al and I met them at my last hospital appointment, (I guess I didn't always come to the hospital by myself), but hadn't put their names and faces together.

My husband mentioned he thought he recognized Ralph from somewhere, but later as Al and I pondered about our short meeting with them, we still hadn't put two and two together. I probably didn't recognize Alvina because she had lost her hair. Besides, the last time we saw them was 30 years earlier when Ralph did the photography at our wedding! I knew them well from Victoria when I was attending university there. At this moment my ears and eyes were opened to the friendship and support I needed that day.

"Do you mind if we open the curtain?" I asked, facing the curtain.

"Not at all," replied Ralph.

As he parted the curtain, they both looked and smiled politely at me in silence for a moment.

I broke the awkwardness, "I know who you are...!"

They were as surprised as I was.

It didn't take us long to catch up on how we got to where we were in this place together. Alvina and I could empathize with each other's battles. We had a great reunion that morning, lots of tears of joy and hardship, but I received the friendship and support that I longed for that morning.

That same week my sister Joy and her husband Alan came to visit. My hair was starting to look scraggly as it continued to fall out; such a timely visit for me; I didn't have to go through the trauma of losing my hair alone. Joy and I found some scissors in the house and brought a kitchen chair into the back yard. As she cut, Alan showed up modeling my wig. We all broke out into a much needed laugh.

My new short haircut cleaned up the straggles. It looked much better, even as I gradually lost my hair completely.

During my time in Vancouver, my husband Al had faithfully driven back and forth every weekend from Penticton to Vancouver to see me. He would leave right after work early Saturday afternoon and arrive that evening. Where did he get the continuous energy required to drive out after a physically and mentally exhausting work week? We spent a few waking hours Saturday evenings and Sunday mornings together before he'd head back home to be at work for Monday morning for 2:00 a.m. (He even made a couple of surprise day trip visits mid-week.) These short, weekly visits with Al, (occasionally one of our kids would come along), and many texts and phone calls were how I communicated with my family while I was in Vancouver.

Now here I was, admitted back at VGH. I never imagined that I would be on the fifteenth floor of the Jim Pattison Pavilion again, especially in the condition I was, and starting all over again. Looking back, it was hard enough going through it once. Now I was back to square one, except this time my condition was critical. But, as all these memories came back to me, I knew I was never alone. Little did I realize how difficult life would become, but for now, I had peace and strength. God, Who was with me in the fall, would be with me again in the journey ahead.

6

ANOTHER HICKMAN LINE

AT VGH AN ONCOLOGY DOCTOR in training is called a fellow. Fellows work together with the hematologist, mine being Doctor Smith, and put a customized medical plan together for each patient. The fellow administers the plan to the patient and sees the patient on a daily basis.

I was very weak and feeling discouraged as I lay in my bed back at Vancouver General Hospital. But the appearance of the fellow that tended to me shortly after I arrived into my room distracted me momentarily from my situation and made me smile. He was a small, bearded, and hunched over man wearing his glasses on the end of his nose, much younger than what first impressions may have revealed. He stood over me in his white cloak holding his clipboard. I was finishing off an orange that I had brought with me from Penticton Regional Hospital.

The fellow was reading off a list of questions and information from his clipboard to me, which I wasn't paying much attention to. But he did catch my attention when he said I would not be eating food for a while. I decided to continue sucking, (and savoring), my last few orange segments, slipping each piece under the clip board with him unaware. (Carolyn smirked at my slickness.) It would be my last bit of solid food for some time.

"You can have ice chips to moisten your mouth when it feels dry," I heard him say.

Doctor Smith didn't make an appearance very often during my hospital stays, but he was there to see me the day after I arrived. I felt very emotional as he entered my room, reminded of the seriousness of my illness in the comfort of his presence. He understood my level of exhaustion, weakness, and vulnerable state. He was the specialist I was used to for overseeing my care.

"You are completely dehydrated and malnourished. You have been very sick," he explained slowly, seriously, looking directly into my eyes. "We are taking you off of food so your bowels have time to recover. We will insert a Hickman line later today so we can start you on an IV nutrition bag."

He continued with understanding, "I'm sure it was hard for you to have to leave your family again and come back here, but this is the best place for you to be looked after."

I listened and, when he left, cried. I knew everything he said was true.

How I wished I was still home and not in this horrible condition. But being so weak and exhausted, even crying and thinking about my situation took a lot of effort. Most of my time was spent just lying in bed; not thinking about much at all.

A Hickman line is a hollow flexible tube inserted above your breast used as a long term intravenous catheter. It is used to draw blood and infuse chemotherapy, antibiotics, blood products, and other medications. For me it meant no more needles! A great relief; when otherwise it would have meant several needles a day. When I had my first Hickman line inserted last September, the doctor assured me I would be given some "I don't care" medication prior to the procedure. That's exactly what it felt like. I was partially aware of the surgery, but I really didn't care.

However this time, I did care. I had an uneasy feeling about the procedure right from the start.

As I was transported into the operating room, I realized how helpless and weak I was this time. I desperately needed the surgeon to recognize my fragility as well. "Be careful with me. I'm very weak and can't take much...," my frail voice cautiously suggested. It was all I could think to say at the moment.

The surgeon casually introduced him and those in the room, and explained that they do this all the time. He assured me that it would be over before I knew it; which was not the case at all! I soon realized I had not been given enough sedative and pain medication as I was aware of everything happening around me.

First, a light blue colored paper towel was put over my face. I could hear the medical team small talking to each other, joking, and discussing their weekend plans. It irritated me. I wanted to pull the paper towel off of me and tell them to concentrate on what they were doing! But, I had been given just enough sedative to not allow my body to cooperate or my mouth to speak.

Then I felt aggressive and painful pulling, pressing, and pounding on my chest... "Why is he being so rough?!" my mind struggled to think clearly. I wanted to fight back, scream out, and escape the pain, but my body lay helpless, trembling, tense, and struggling to battle the horrific ordeal.

Parts of a verse from the Bible came to mind, "...I am with you...I will strengthen you and help you; I will uphold you with my righteous right hand." (1)

I desperately struggled to mentally focus and cling on to the verse; a promise...but was constantly distracted by rough pulling, pressing, and pounding.

"Hold my hand!" I yelled in my head. "I don't feel Your Hand!" I'd recite the verse again, hanging on to it to help me endure the agonizing 20 minute procedure.

During his next visit the fellow inspected my Hickman line and commented on how good it looked. I was pleasantly surprised to hear that, but I decided it was best not to know what goes on during a surgery and to have plenty of "I don't care" medication.

7

A NEW ROOM AND GOOD SHIT

WHEN I WAS FIRST ADMITTED back at VGH, I was tested for the contagious bacteria, C diff., in my stool. For that reason, I was the sole user of the shared bathroom; my roommate inconvenienced by having to use a different one. So when a private room and bathroom became available I was moved in. Until the results came back negative, anyone, including medical staff or visitors, had to dress into a gown and wear gloves before entering my room.

The possibility of having C diff. moved me to a beautiful room! The large window in my room and the almost floor to ceiling window in my private bathroom were facing East. Many mornings as the sky brightened and turned pink, I'd sit up in my bed and watch the sun make its way over the snow-topped distant mountains. In my picture window was Burnaby Mountain, Central Park, and on cloudless days, far in the distance, Mt. Baker. The vast window in my bathroom allowed me to enjoy the outside view while showering and tending to nature. But I was glad I never met up with a window washer during those times. (My window was missing a covering.)

A few days later the results came back negative; I could be moved into a shared room any day. But each day I remained. (The nurses reminded me how fortunate I was to have my private room.)

I heard the results of my stool sample while Al and Carolyn were heading back to Penticton from visiting me. I texted Al right away; he was always eager to hear any good news. I didn't hear from him for a while as he was driving in an "out of service" area. In the meantime I had forgotten all about the text I had sent him.

So when I did get his reply and read, "You're a good shit." I struggled to make sense of his brazen salutation.

"Where did that come from...?" I'd give him a piece of my mind as soon as I figured he was home.

Carolyn picked up the phone.

"What's with Dad? Do you know what he texted me?" (I forgot to say "hello".) "He was so rude."

"Oh. That was me, Mom. I texted you on his phone because he was driving..."

"Why would you text me that?" I barked back.

"Dad told me to...", (her usual tattle-tale response.) "It was a joke, Mom!. We were celebrating your stool results!"

"Oh." I was still mad, "Well, it wasn't funny."

But it was.

MORE HOSPITAL DAYS

"NOW THAT YOUR HICKMAN LINE is inserted, we can hook your nutrition bag up. You'll have one bag every twelve hours and the other bag once every evening. You can still eat ice chips," the nurse explained with forced enthusiasm, hoping it was contagious.

It wasn't. I watched her hook a bag up on my IV pole that looked like pee, and another bag like coffee cream.

My daughter Carolyn was able to stay in Vancouver with me a lot of the time for the first while. She was finishing her term at university and any time she had some days off she would head down to Vancouver. She stayed at Grandma's house at night and would spend much of her time with me in the hospital. She was great company, a real strength for me, and she enjoyed the hospital atmosphere; she was finishing her third year of nursing school.

While I continued sucking on ice chips, Carolyn would head off to West Broadway a couple of times a day and try out some eating places. When she'd return I'd interview her on the details of her eating experience. "Where did you go? What did you have? What did it taste like...?"

Sometimes she'd bring food back with her. I'd snoop through her take-out bag. Even though I couldn't eat or even taste a morsel of it, I enjoyed dissecting, sniffing, and discussing it. I could only imagine the taste and texture in my mouth. While I was deprived of food it became the next best thing to eating; that and watching cooking shows.

Carolyn brought her lap top to the hospital so we could watch shows together. We'd both sit up on my bed with her lap top propped up in front of us. My preference was the cooking shows. Master Chef Canada became one of my favorites. I also discovered the food channel on the TV in the patient lounge and would head down there when I was alone. Sometimes while I was watching, I wrote notes, wanting to remember helpful tips and cooking ideas. I looked forward to the day that I could use the notes at home and cook for my family again.

But writing was a difficult task for me. The medication I was on made my hands shaky; my writing was messy and barely legible. My brain struggled too as I jotted a few words here and there, trying to keep up with watching the show as I wrote. I didn't want to miss anything. It was a good challenge for me.

Carolyn quickly grew tired of cooking shows, but for me it was as close to eating as I could get!

I spent most of each day in my bed, except for the few routine activities that I struggled to accomplish. It was very important for me to walk around the ward every day if I could; it would help maintain and preserve some of my mobility. The high doses of medication, especially the prednisone, caused muscle atrophy.

Although I was no longer on solid food, the diarrhea continued. I was given a plastic hat, (so it was called), to use in the toilet to measure the volume of my diarrhea. A chart was attached to the bathroom door where I recorded my results. That and other simple tasks like washing myself and brushing my teeth were monumental for me. On more energetic days I changed out of the hospital gown into my own clothes and occasionally made my bed.

I requested our big, heavy world atlas book from home. It was a good way to pass the time. I enjoyed looking at countries around the world and their major cities.

I had a white board on the wall across from my bed. To keep me informed, the nurse recorded my daily blood counts and wrote his or her name on it for that particular day. But Carolyn decided to use the white board, (every square inch of it), for listing countries and their capital cities. It was much more interesting than daily blood counts. Plus, I knew most of the nurses' names by then anyway. While I sat up in bed, she quizzed me on the country and capital city names every day until I got 100%. Then I graduated to a new set of countries. It was good for my brain and gave us something productive to do together. Other than that, a bit of texting, the occasional short phone call, and the day was done.

Carolyn was helpful on days when even small tasks were too difficult for me, but I mostly thrived on her affection. I found comfort and security as she often joined me on my bed, holding my hand, linking arms with me, and just being close. Our roles had changed. She had become the strength and security that I needed in my vulnerable state.

Once a nurse entering my room was momentarily thrown off...two patients on one bed? Her bewildered look told me it wasn't appropriate or hygienic or something...

"That's not a good idea." She blurted out. "You could catch a virus or bacteria from one another."

We chuckled at her response and continued sharing my bed. Carolyn's affection was too important for me to give up.

I had continual and intense abdominal pain from the GVHD of my gut. I was first given oral medication which was upped to subcutaneous, a needle poked into the fat of my stomach. It was faster relief than oral medication but the pain still wasn't managed well and resulted in struggling days. Once my Hickman line was inserted, the most effective pain medication was a narcotic given through my line. It was fast acting, took the pain completely away, but had a short duration. As soon as I felt the pain return, I pressed the call bell to get a nurse. She would come and ask me my level of pain. Then she would draw up and prepare the appropriate dose of medication. By the time the medication was administered and I received relief, it often took up to 45 minutes. I remember many times, agonizing through the pain, while the nurse hooked up the medication to my IV.

Once when my nurse returned with pain medication and was busily hooking it up as quickly as she could, the sound of my fingers tapping the railing on the side of my bed caught her attention. She looked over at me; my face was buried in my pillow and my body tense as I endured the pain.

"The distress is too much," she observed. "I'm going to get something done about that," I heard her tell herself as she left my room.

A couple of days later, I was hooked up to a Patient Controlled Analgesia (PCA) machine that attached to my IV pole. Now I controlled the relief I needed for my pain. I just pressed a button on the PCA machine and a dose of hydromorphone immediately flowed through my Hickman line into my blood stream. The pain relief happened within about twenty seconds: almost unbelievable. My pain was finally and continually under control.

THE ATG PLAN, PREDNISONE, AND REAL FOOD

AFTER A COUPLE OF WEEKS of ice chips, my bowels got the rest they needed and I was started on a clear liquid diet. Now I had something to look forward to three times a day; well I did for the first few days. I started with jelly cubes, warm decaf coffee or tea, and apple juice every meal. For lunch and dinner warm chicken or beef broth was added. The chicken broth had a bit of flavor, but the beef broth tasted like salt water. The juice and jelly were a sugar overdose, so I mostly slurped the chicken broth and drank water. When a visitor asked if they could bring me anything, I requested hot bone marrow broth in a thermos. It didn't sound appetizing, but I knew it was nutritious and much tastier than salt water. Before long, I had a room full of empty thermoses.

A week later I started on full fluids. For breakfast I had warm, watery cream of wheat, milk, yogurt, and juice. For lunch and dinner, I either had canned tomato, or cream of mushroom soup, (without the mushrooms), yogurt, milk, juice, and pudding. It was a treat for the first few days.

Soon after, meal time didn't appeal to me anymore; especially when one particular pudding showed up on my tray. "Not again." The top layer was rubbery; I had to break through it with a plastic spoon to get to the creamy part, but it was flavorless. "No thanks."

Unfortunately, with this gradual introduction to food, my bowels began to act up again. There was also blood in my diarrhea and my hemoglobin dropped to critical levels. I began receiving blood transfusions on a regular basis.

The fellow came in one day and sat down next to my bed to explain, "Your condition is not improving. We have to try a new plan. Your GVHD will worsen unless we start you on Anti-Thymocyte Globulin, in other words, the ATG treatment plan. This is a more intense medication that we need to administer in order to get your bowels working properly..."

The more intense medication part scared me! Thoughts thrashed around in my head like a violent storm. "This is not good news, but what else can they do? Why isn't my body responding? More medication can't be good; my body is suffering terribly as it is. What if this new plan doesn't work? ATG? What do the letters stand for? Did he say something about the side effects? I can't remember. Was my brain even working properly anymore? Does anyone know what I feel like, or what I'm going through?!"

I wanted to scream and cry out, but I didn't have the strength, so I just lay there. I wanted to wake up from this crazy nightmare, but that didn't happen either.

Well the ATG treatment sure took its toll on my body and it only took a couple of weeks to feel the change. I especially noticed the loss of strength in my legs and arms. My legs felt very heavy whenever I moved them on my bed. An enormous effort was required just to get myself off the bed and onto my feet. My arms felt like everything I picked up was much heavier than before. I needed both hands just to lift the plate of food off my tray. My muscles were rapidly deteriorating from the medication.

Whenever I raised the top half of my bed so I could be in a sitting position, my body gradually slid down and became slumped into the bend of the bed. I didn't have enough strength to pull myself back up, so I'd press the call bell for a nurse to come to my rescue.

She'd call another nurse to help. They would both stand at the head of my bed, one on each side.

"One, two, three, pull," one of the nurses would call out.

Together they would both pull the bed sheet I lay on back up the bed to bring me into a comfortable upright position again. I used the call bell many times a day, just for that reason. I always kept the call bell within reach. In fact, I made sure that everything I needed each day was in arms reach, otherwise I would be continually calling for help. There was very little I could do on my own. I became completely dependent on others to take care of me.

Although the ATG plan seemed very destructive on my body, it was only a four week plan. The prednisone, however, (one of the main anti-rejection medications I was prescribed for the GVHD), was a much longer term drug and very destructive. Because my GVHD was so intense, I was on the highest dose of prednisone prescribed for my body weight, 130 mg a day, and for long periods of time.

Prednisone was causing my body to retain a lot of fluid. My face puffed up, changing my facial looks completely. The swelling made my nose look smaller and pointy. My mouth also looked smaller because it was squished between two puffy cheeks. My eyes looked bigger, bulged out, and ached from the pressure of the retained fluid. The swelling rid me of all my facial crow's feet. My neck looked like a stretched out water balloon, jiggling when I talked or nodded.

My abdomen was also swollen with retained fluid, putting pressure on my lungs which sometimes made it hard to breathe comfortably. I'd often arch my back and drop my head back just to get a proper full breath of air.

My ankles and feet swelled to about three times their normal size; edema. The largest size socks the hospital provided were far too small and cut off my circulation. Instead, I wore extra-large Alpaca socks that were brought from home. They were very comfortable; loose on my feet and kept my cold feet warm. I would elevate my feet up on pillows whenever possible. This would help alleviate pressure from the fluid constantly accumulating in them. Visitors would sit on my bed and massage the retained fluid back up into my legs. Sometimes a watery fluid would ooze out of the pores of my feet from the pressure.

Although some parts of my body were very swollen with retained fluid, other parts were wasting away. The high dose of prednisone was breaking down my major muscle areas, especially in my arms, hips, buttocks, and legs.

"Your butt's missing, Mom." Carolyn humored.

"I know. All the diarrhea;I must have pooped it off somewhere." I added to the silliness.

"Let's put up a WANTED poster for your missing buttocks." Carolyn laughed as we slowly walked.

Then there were my skinny legs. Where did all the muscles go on my once strong legs?

Carolyn joked some more, "Mom, you're lucky, most teens would envy your thigh gap."

I was able to momentarily joke lightly about my new body type, but deep down I worried about the severity of my condition and my deteriorating body strength.

On good days, usually after I had a blood transfusion and my energy level was up, I was encouraged to walk around the ward to help keep me mobile and work against atrophy. And so I walked religiously, knowing it was all and everything I could do to help myself.

Prednisone also caused my skin to become very thin, fragile, wrinkly and saggy. My wrists were getting smaller and my arms looked long and skinny with thin, wrinkly skin hanging down.

It had become very obvious that all the medication was wreaking havoc on my body. I had lost about twenty-five pounds in a month. Some of the same staff on the ward that had cared for me in the fall now didn't recognize me.

One day my Uncle Walter and Auntie Betty came by. I recognized them as they stopped by my door way to check the room number.

"Oh good; company." I thought from my bed as they entered. But in a moment, after looking around at my roommate and me, they turned away, leaving.

"Come back. It's me, Marge." I forced out, my voice strained and weak.

My platelets, the clotting blood cells, were often very low. The slightest little pinch or bump caused bleeding under my skin. I noticed dark purple blotches. Where did they come from? I continually accumulated more.

I was often cold in the hospital because my circulation was poor and my blood counts were usually low. (A fan controlling the air quality in my room also blew nonstop above my bed.) I kept layers of hospital blankets on me, but they weighed heavily as they draped over my frail body.

My family brought me light, fluffy blankets and warm, flannel pajamas. I kept my Alpaca socks on all the time, wore a toque and long sleeved sweaters. Aaahh; much better.

My hair had already started to grow back in: grey and thin, with frizzy curls. My kids bought me stylish head bands; I wore them every day. They controlled my frizz, kept my head warm, and looked more stylish than my toque!

If someone came to visit that hadn't seen me for a while, I warned them that I looked a little different than I used to. Sometimes I felt self-conscious about the way I looked. But few mentioned it. And if they did, the only comments were, "You look good..."

"Why do they say that? I know what I look like." I wondered to myself.

With the ATG plan now in progress, the medical team decided it was time to introduce me to a food diet again, starting with clear fluids. Within a couple of weeks I started on a low fiber diet. Added to my breakfast choices from before were a piece of warm, white bread and boiled or scrambled eggs. For lunch I usually had a white bread sandwich with a morsel of roast beef, turkey, or egg in it, along with either canned tomato or mushroom soup. Dinner consisted of pork, chicken, or fish, instant mashed potatoes smothered in salty gravy, or occasionally white rice, and an over-cooked, soggy vegetable choice. Boost was also an option to increase my calorie intake but it was too sweet. Mixing it with milk helped a little.

In the fall, I enjoyed and looked forward to my hospital meals. I liked the novelty of having them prepared for me with no clean up on my part. But not anymore.

10

VISITORS AND DAY PASSES

AN IMPORTANT PART OF MY journey in Vancouver was my constant connection with family, relatives, and friends. As I look back in my journal, my good days always included company. Although I was very weak and often discouraged, I gained strength and cheered up immensely when I had someone coming to visit. Texting was so convenient for communicating and arranging visits.

Many relatives and friends living in the Greater Vancouver area visited me regularly. My cousin Ken worked close to the hospital and faithfully came to visit me after work. I enjoyed listening to him talk about his family life; what he was barbecuing for dinner or what their plans were for the weekend. Our conversations made me feel connected to a once familiar life style.

My niece Shannon, (aka Shaggy), came one late afternoon, just after my sister-in-law Violet had dropped off a sample of this and that from a restaurant she had eaten at earlier that day.

"Hey Shaggy, want to stay for dinner?"

She set up two chairs and rolled my bed table between them, right next to my window. With my tray of hospital food and Violet's tasty treats, a small feast lay before us. Enjoying the view of Vancouver through my window while we dined made it seem fancy. It was a special meal time for me; some delicious food in good company.

When my brother, Rob, wasn't out of town, he visited me regularly and often brought me food. (I craved many foods; anything other than hospital foods, and depended on others to bring them.)

Once he brought me a big, juicy, delicious, (homemade patty), barbecued burger on a white, soft, freshly baked bun. I remember the details and savored the flavor! (I requested chicken wings from KFC once. Instead Al brought me chicken strips. It was hard for me to conceal my disappointment.)

My sister-in-law Heather, (Al's sister), often came to visit me as well. She took the bus and sky train to spend the day with me. She would massage the fluid from my feet back up into my legs, walk the ward with me if I had the strength, listen to me, allow my tears, encourage me, and snuggle with me when I felt vulnerable and emotional. I desperately needed and depended on her care and affection.

Al faithfully came every weekend and Carolyn stayed for days at a time. And there were many others: I had a constant circle of support around me. Although I didn't want to inconvenience people as they took time to come see me, I didn't dare turn any offers down. I couldn't because I knew how gravely their involvement in my life kept me afloat day by day.

There were a few occasions I was given a short day pass. Even if it was only for an hour, I could hardly contain my excitement. As soon as I got the OK to leave the hospital my energy level instantly jumped. Going outside into the real world and fresh air meant everything to me. I think the fellows knew what was good for my soul was good for my healing.

But it was a high maintenance job for any family member to take on. Everything had to be just right. First, I had to get the OK from the fellow working that day. The nurse had to make sure I had enough pain medication for the duration of the outing. And finding an available wheelchair wasn't always a simple task. Pillows had to be arranged just right in my wheelchair for comfort, my IV pole had to be disconnected, a trip to the bathroom, and an extra sweater and blanket; they were all part of the preparations. Then I would plop myself in my wheelchair for "Marge's Big Day Out". I would sign out at the front desk, put a mask over my mouth and nose, and head down the crowded elevator; fifteen floors down, through the busy walkways, and finally out the automatic sliding glass hospital doors.

Outside, I'd remove my mask, extend my heavy arms into the air, and squeal out, "Freedom."

It was usually my husband or kids that pushed me in my wheelchair. I never came back a minute early. Sometimes I pushed the time a bit longer, but not too much; I didn't want to risk any chance of not being granted another outing. My wheelchair drivers were put to the test, pushing me around, up and down some steep hills, gravel, and long distances.

I happily coached them on. "Turn here...watch out...go faster...slow down..."

My outings included Grandville Island, up and down West Broadway, Charleson Park, another park across from the hospital, and City Square; depending on how much time I was permitted and the fitness level of my wheelchair driver.

11

TO GRANDMA'S HOUSE WITH LAURA

THE ATG TREATMENT PLAN STARTED to work; my bowels stabilized. Now that I was on a full diet, I gained strength as well. I was told I would be discharged in a couple of days.

I was really nervous and anxious about the thought, even though I knew it was a step in the right direction. Going back to Grandma's house this time was a lot different. I now required twenty-four-seven care and it needed to come from someone I felt completely comfortable and safe with. I was used to the care I received in the hospital. Everything was set up for me there. How would anybody else even begin to know how to look after me?

It seemed going to Grandma's house would be a huge undertaking for me and for whoever would look after me. There was so much to think about and figure out.

My mind was flooded with many thoughts and questions. First, I didn't know how I would even get into the house. There were two steps that led to the sidewalk that led to six more steps to the front door. I knew my legs were not strong enough to get me up. I would also need someone to drive me to the hospital three days a week for treatment and observation. In the fall, I depended on the Mason volunteer driver's program, but now I wasn't able to get in and out of the car myself; I needed a different option.

One concern led to another. I would have to arrange my appointments at the hospital, remember them, and get there on time. In the hospital, my appointments were all arranged for me and I was either transported by bed or wheelchair.

My concerns continued. Who would prepare low fiber, nutritious meals for me? And living in Violet's house, I needed someone to do dishes, laundry, and housekeeping. I wasn't capable of doing any of it myself.

What about my medications? At the hospital the nurses looked after them for me; making sure they were the right ones, the right doses at the right times; even delivering them to me in a little paper cup for goodness sake! Now I would be responsible for all that; AND getting them from the pharmacy! I would need to know what each one was, how much to take, and how often, every day. There were so many pills! What if I ever forgot to take one...?

The more I thought about it, the more the questions and concerns bombarded me. Oh! What about the bathroom? I would also have to get in and out of a tub and bathe myself. What would I hold onto? Even getting me off the toilet would be a challenge; especially without railings to grab onto like I had in the hospital. Getting on and off chairs and couches in the house without assistance would be impossible.

I imagined myself being completely helpless in every way at Grandma's house and if I didn't have the appropriate care that I needed, well, my very life was at stake. When these thoughts chased me, I felt overwhelmed and stressed out; exhausted too. There was too much to figure out.

I walked around the ward one day, realizing how slow my walking had become, how heavy and sluggish my body felt as I held onto my IV pole. I felt the extra burden of how I would handle being at Grandma's house.

As I walked, I brought my burden to God. "This is too much for me. I don't know what to do...I need help. I need Your help."

As I came around the last corner towards my room, the thought came to me, "You helped me through everything so far up to now. I don't have to figure it out. You have to. I have to trust You."

I felt physically lighter; a huge burden instantly lifted off my shoulders. I knew at that moment He heard me. And then in my head I heard, "I will work things out for you. Don't worry. Take one day at a time."

I walked back to my room feeling a new peace inside. I had only one option; simply trust.

The physiotherapist came in to see me the next day. "I heard the good news. You're being discharged in a couple of days."

I still wasn't sure if it was good news.

"Let's talk about any concerns you might have about how you will be able to get around in the house."

"Oh, yes. I have lots of concerns." They were fresh in my mind, so I explained them all to her.

She took me to the exercise room where I practiced going up stairs. She showed me which leg to use for going up the stairs and which leg to use for going down. I learned how to use the railing to help pull me up, while she gave me a push up from my bottom.

"I'll be back to practice the stairs with you again tomorrow. The practice will give you the confidence you'll need when you leave the hospital. I'll also have the occupational therapist come in and talk about any equipment you might need to help you get around in the house." Then she left my room.

"That went well," I thought as I remembered my conversation with God...

I had connected with an old high school friend when I had my transplant in the fall. She went by "Baerg" in high school, (her last name). But when we reconnected in Vancouver, I thought of her as my angel. She lived in North Van and was excited I called her up. She had Wednesdays off, so most of those days she picked me up from Grandma's house and took me to different places in and around Vancouver. (I relied on others to get me out of the house.) Since returning to VGH, we texted back and forth and she came to visit me at the hospital regularly. I texted her to let her know I was being discharged and was heading back to Grandma's house.

"When? We'll need to get equipment for you to get around the house," she texted back.

Baerg is a physiotherapist. She spends her working day driving to her clients' homes, making sure they have the equipment they need for safety, and supports them in many ways needed while living at home.

She came after work that day to discuss all the equipment she could either get from the Red Cross or had available through her work for me. She had more than just the basics. Something as simple as a handle that you take with you and attach to any car to help boost you in and out was so handy! (I recently saw advertisements of that handy gadget on TV.)

She also reminded me I would need a rail to get out of bed. (At the hospital, a press of a button can lift the top half of the bed up, to sit up or get out of bed, or lowers you down to rest.) It would be difficult to get myself up and out of a regular bed. But with a rail on the side of the bed, I would be able to grab onto it like a handle and pull myself up using my arms. Then, when in a sitting position, I could rotate my legs to the side, drop them to the floor, and stand up.

I would also need a commode; it's like a tall chair that extends over the toilet. With no muscle in my legs, it would help me get up from using the toilet because I didn't have a railing on the wall to use to help pull me up.

A bench in the bath tub to sit on for my shower, a wheel chair for walks outside, and a walker for in the house were also necessary pieces of equipment. Baerg also brought me this cool pop-up chair device. I could put it down anywhere I wanted to sit and it would pop me up as I needed the boost to get up.

"I can fit the equipment I have available in my car. I'll pick up the rest from the Red Cross and bring them to the house for when you get there. What day are you going to Grandma's house?"

"I was told Wednesday morning," I answered.

"Perfect, that's my day off. I'll stop in your room in the morning. You'll also need to get your medication. We can pick it up together and then I'll take you to Grandma's house. It'll be an exhausting day for you, just to get you settled in. I'm glad I'll be off that day."

"Wow, thanks," was all I could say as I shook my head in disbelief.

I also got a text that day. It was my friend Laura from Medicine Hat, asking when it would be a good time to come and help me.

I texted her back, "Now would be a perfect time."

"I'll book a flight and come out. I can use my air miles and rent a car too. It's just that it usually takes about a week or two to get a flight, but I'll let you know."

She had no idea how frail I was, and how desperately I needed and wanted her to come.

She phoned the next day, "I can't believe it. I've got a flight booked for Wednesday. I arrive in Vancouver at 8:00 a.m. After I get my luggage and rent a car, I should get to the hospital by around 10:00 a.m. Will that work?"

"Are you sure you can get away and do this? ...yeah, that will work out great." I put my cell phone down bewildered about how everything came together; beyond what I could have arranged.

Laura and I have been very good friends for many years. I would feel completely safe and secure with her, especially with all her care giving experience. She had taken care of her grandfather years ago for several months before he passed away. Presently, she was helping her daughter look after her triplets.

I humbly said, "Thank You." Just thinking about how everything came together brought tears streaming down my face. He really did figure it all out for me.

Wednesday morning Laura arrived about 10:00 a.m. The doctor came in, gave me instructions on my medications, any symptoms that I needed to look out for, and the contact numbers I needed in case of an emergency. I was glad Laura was there to hear all the information. Although it wasn't much, it easily overwhelmed me and I didn't want to miss any of the details.

Shortly after, Baerg arrived and together they packed up all my belongings. All I had to do was get in and out of the car using the special handle and Laura's help. Then the stairs; I put my strong leg on the first step, grabbed the rail with my arms, pulled with all my might, and with a push under my butt, I was able to get up each step one by one and into the house. Baerg was right; that was exhausting.

While Laura picked up some groceries, I sat on the pop-up chair in the living room thinking, "If there was ever an emergency, I would be completely helpless...trying to get myself out of Grandma's house, if it wasn't for the pop-up chair; a simple, but ingenious invention." Thinking about my vulnerable state sent shivers up my spine.

Laura prepared dinner, the first of low-fiber, healthy, delicious meals.

I rested, enjoyed peaceful moments, and contently soaked up the familiar surroundings of Grandma's house from the fall: the antique wood smell, old upholstered furniture, hardwood floors extending out from large, wool woven area rugs, arched entry ways, heavy drapes outlining the living and dining room windows, large paintings and other wall décor depicting Hungarian culture, and precious rare ornaments adorning furniture tops...and the rustic, wood front entrance door. It had a small rod iron framed window and door at eye level that I remember playfully opening and peering through as company arrived. From the outside, Grandma's house reminded me of a friendly-looking gingerbread house.

The next morning started like many others would for the next couple of weeks. Laura and I would sit at the kitchen table together where she'd help me organize my medications for the day.

"How would you like your egg today?" Laura would offer. "...poached, scrambled...?"

She'd prepare an egg, fresh sourdough white bread from Stong's bakery with butter and freshly made strawberry jam, and a glass of almond milk. I loved breakfast; a hundred times better than the hospital. Then I would down oodles of pills.

Days I didn't have appointments continued with Laura visiting me in my room. She'd come and sit in the fancy queen chair that was in the corner of my room while I lay comfortably on my bed, relaxed, and with little pain. It was a favorite part of my day.

After breakfast, medications, and a visit, I would have a shower. Sometimes, that was enough for the bed to call me back for a morning nap. I gradually worked up to doing a few small chores; making my bed, washing a few dishes, and sometimes getting my lunch ready for my hospital trip the next day. We sat on the deck in the back on sunny days and Laura drove us to Spanish Banks and Pacific Spirit Park. We took small walks around the neighborhood and occasionally had a coffee at the local coffee shop. Well Laura did. Coffee wasn't a choice drink for my health, so Laura always got an extra cup and put a slurp of coffee with cream in it for me.

I enjoyed Laura's homemade soups and healthy smoothies for lunch and always looked forward to another delicious gourmet meal for dinner. I would get comfortable in my sofa chair in the living room, turn the TV on, and she would bring me my plate of dinner. It always looked like it came from a fancy restaurant. We borrowed some movies from the local library for evening entertainment.

On my hospital days, I packed myself up for the day. Most patients found any available vinyl, reclining chair in one of the rooms with two or three others. I remembered the procedure well from the fall. I often noticed and passed by a couple of rooms with a single bed and private bathroom. They were reserved for patients requiring more care and assistance. Now I was one of those.

"I'll need a room reserved for me with a bed and commode; for every appointment," I requested from my nurse. She quickly accommodated me with the special needs I required and left a note on my file for each of my appointments. I was too frail and weak to be sitting up in a chair, especially because I was often there for several hours, depending on what products I needed that day.

I began my routine as I had in the fall: checked my name off on the white board wall schedule that faced the nursing station, weighed in, picked up my clip board and a water bottle, and put my name on the outside of the door of the room reserved for me so the nurse knew I had arrived. Then I wheeled an available vitals instrument into my room. To prevent any spreading of germs, I put on disposable gloves and wiped everything that I was touching with disposable wipes. I took my vitals: blood pressure, temperature, heart rate, and oxygen level, and recorded them on the sheet on the clip board. The nurse took blood samples from me, sent them off to determine what blood products and/or electrolytes I needed, and transmitted them through my Hickman line. I was left with the continued responsibility of taking and recording my vitals during specific time intervals. Occasionally, I got myself up to use the bathroom and took my IV pole for a walk down the hall for exercise. Most of my day was spent resting, watching a bit of TV, and visiting with Laura.

Laura usually stayed with me at the hospital. She was very relaxed; never impatient, frustrated or bored with me. She stayed no matter how long the day looked and never complained. She'd go downstairs for a coffee always bringing me a small sample. She was enjoying her time in Vancouver as if it was a holiday.

Laura had arranged to stay a week with me. I had no idea who would look after me when she left, but I learned to live one day at a time. Worrying about a few days ahead took too much energy.

During one of my appointments and towards the end of her week's stay, Laura quietly left my hospital room with her cell phone in hand. She returned a few minutes later. "I talked to Dave, (her husband), and Mallory, (her daughter). ...they said it would be OK for me to stay another week. Mallory said she'd figure something out for her triplets' care and Dave said, 'you need me more than he does...'"

"Thanks", was all I could offer and meant it more than she could ever know.

However, Laura's holiday in Vancouver began to turn sour towards the end of her second week. I was becoming very impatient with my condition and frustrated that I had to be in Vancouver for so long. Initially Doctor Smith mentioned that June would be a reasonable goal for me to be home. But now it was already mid- May and we both knew that June was no longer realistic. Even so, it was difficult for me to accept.

I vented out at God. "Why should Laura have to come all the way from Medicine Hat, disrupt her family commitments to look after me? Why is it taking so long for me to get better?"

The prednisone drug was beginning to show its ugly effects on my emotions. I was easily angered, and irritated, and felt I didn't have any control over my life. I was bossy, critical, and adamant about silly, little things, demanding my way or the highway.

I often couldn't keep my rage bottled up inside. I would sit up in my bed at Grandma's house, lean back on the head board, and scream into my pillow, muffling the noise. Other times I didn't care about using the pillow to hide my anger and I would just yell out into the air. I felt powerful as I held nothing back and heard the angry strength of my voice shrill through the house.

It wasn't just random screaming. I was unleashing angry words at God. Maybe because I didn't think He was listening and needed to get His attention. Or maybe because He was much greater and bigger than me, and could handle my venting; I knew He wouldn't yell back or judge me. Or maybe because I was completely helpless and knew He was the only One who could do something about my situation.

Hearing me scream out from my room disturbed Laura; knowing there was nothing she could do to change what I was going through. I'd even be short with her out of frustration and then not care how it made her feel.

One day I got out of the car from a day at the hospital with Laura. I struggled up the first two steps, always having to depend on that little push from behind, and lost my temper. Using every little muscle in me, I pushed my walker over and crawled on all fours on the cement sidewalk.

"I'm going to do this myself! I don't want your help!" I hollered.

Concerned, Laura gently warned me to stop so I wouldn't hurt myself. She knew my platelets were low and I could easily scrape my knees and start bleeding badly, making my situation much worse.

I yelled back at her, "I don't care!" and kept crawling, wailing loudly with anger and frustration at my helpless condition.

Even if I did apologize, Laura knew there would probably be more incidents. The twenty-four seven physical care that she gave me wasn't nearly as difficult as was dealing with my behavior.

One of the doctors who had spent a lot of time with me came into my room one day. She knew the length of time I was in Vancouver was wearing on me, that my drugs were having a bad effect on my physical body and emotions, and that my intense struggle of GVHD was making me feel very discouraged. She also knew I was focused on wanting to go home. As I lay on the hospital bed, she came and sat beside me, put her face close to mine and looked into my eyes. She knew I needed to be reminded of the truth.

"Marge, I want you to listen to what I am saying," she began very soberly. "I know how much you miss your family and would like to be home. But if you choose to leave the hospital and go home to Penticton, you will die. No one has the expertise in Penticton that we have here to look after you. I know you're a fighter. You need to refocus, stop thinking about going home."

Then her face brightened as she continued. "We're slowly reducing your prednisone medication. That's good news. Focus on that and getting better. Then you will be able to go home."

When Laura's two weeks were up, I didn't need to wonder who would continue the care giving role for me. After all the effort Laura had put into looking after me so well, it hadn't made any difference on my condition. In fact it worsened. I had an infection in my urine and my diarrhea increased, turning dark green in color again. My prednisone dose was maximized again, and I was admitted back into the hospital.

NO LONGER LIVING

AL CONTINUED TO VISIT ME every weekend, leaving Sunday mornings very discouraged as my condition worsened. He didn't want to bump into people he knew in Penticton anymore in case they would ask about me. There wasn't any good news to share and it just reminded him of how difficult life had become for his family. How long could they all go on like this?

Much of my journal up until now had been about how God had looked after me through this difficult time. I had written many things I was thankful for during this journey and how very specifically and practically God had looked after every little detail of my life in my vulnerable state; I could go on and on; everyday things that anyone would take for granted, except for a person as helpless and dependent as I was.

But now, in my long struggle with a body that was deteriorating with GVHD and medicine that was both keeping me alive and destroying my body, my dialogue with God changed.

I was reading in the Bible, "If you remain in me and my words remain in you, ask whatever you wish, and it will be given you." (2)

I had angry and challenging words to say about that in my journal because my life wasn't turning out the way I was expecting it to. "Well God, I've been asking You to heal me. My family, relatives, friends, and friends of friends...are all praying for my recovery. Are You even listening? And if You are, why aren't You doing something?"

I was frustrated and impatient. My writing continued. "You don't even need the prayers. Jesus healed people all the time. (I've read the Bible stories.) What about me? The medicine is not working. It's just slowly destroying me. How long do I have to live like this before You help me?".

That's the short version of my journal when I was readmitted into the hospital. My writing continued with the same message, just different words. My penmanship was getting larger and messier, sometimes scratching through the paper as I angrily wrote.

I didn't look forward to company when they came like I used to.

My cousin Eunice came to visit. "Marge, you can't give up. Your family wants and needs you.

"I would have looked after my mom forever...," she reflected with sentiment on her season of care giving for my Auntie Mary until she passed on. "Your family wants you no matter what condition you're in."

I didn't like hearing that. "What about me and my suffering? I don't want to just be alive like this for my family. Besides, this is no longer living; rather, slowly dying..."

My Uncle George, Auntie Adelaide, Cousin Annette, and her son, Brad, drove out from Chilliwack the next day to see me.

..."I'll walk you back to the elevator," I offered; and often did as company was leaving.

After sitting on my bed for a while visiting I knew I needed the walk, as short as it was, and as slow as I was. My relatives lumbered along with me at my slow pace as we headed to the elevator, pausing every few short steps, not wanting to rush me in any way. I was reminded of my dire condition; I couldn't even keep up with my elderly aunt and uncle.

And neither could I hold my angry thoughts inside. "Why do I keep on living...?" I bitterly spewed out at them as we waited for the elevator. (The busy elevator often took time coming up fifteen floors.)

"I hate living. I'm angry and mad. I wish I could punch something..." I continued.

"Here, punch my arm." Annette promptly offered, turning her shoulder towards me.

I did; as hard as I could. I knew I didn't have strength to inflict much pain or damage.

"Here, punch Brad." She offered her son's shoulder, bigger and stronger, as he turned his.

I punched his too; many times and harder as my anger turned into strength, gaining momentum.

"You can punch my arm too." My octogenarian Aunt offered, hoping it was helping.

...my elderly aunt? I couldn't...

Punching didn't help anyway; it only broke the awkwardness of my angry outburst momentarily. My struggle was much deeper than what a few punches could fix.

The elevator bell finally dinged; my signal to say farewell to my visitors.

As the elevator doors opened, they turned to enter.

I heard Annette ponder aloud to herself, "There's something wrong with my Mare..." (She was talking about me; we always called each other Mare Schlinker; a character we created during our childhood summers spent together in the raspberry patch.) Her words continued, as she stepped into the elevator. "She's not herself...has she given up...?"

If there was something Annette could have done to help me, she would have; anything.

I knew her heart hurt for me as I watched her turn and walk away with her family, leaving me alone in my critical condition. But I didn't care about how she felt. I had become completely despondent and unappreciative of anyone's care and efforts, including my own.

"Why do people keep coming to visit and care for me?" I wondered, as I slowly made my way back to my room. "It's not making any difference. I'm a bad investment; no need for them to waste their time with me anymore."

In one way I wanted people to move on and forget about me; to get on with their own lives. Yet I desperately, so desperately needed them to stick with me. I needed them in an astronomical way...to encourage and listen to me, to understand and not judge my frustration, anger, and craziness.

As I lay in my hospital bed, I became aware that I was coming to the end of my life. I pondered many thoughts. "Is this really how my life is going to end? What a horrible ending to this journey; it started out so well. My stem cell transplant went so smoothly; you would hardly have known that I went through something so incredible. It was mostly my hair, or lack of, that gave it away. I went home at Christmas and started carrying on with life as I had before the transplant. My brother had been my donor, a perfect match too. He gave everything he could for me, and now, for what? I was going to die anyways. What if he blames himself? Maybe I shouldn't even have had the transplant...

"Plus, my pathetic life is so difficult for my husband. He comes to visit me faithfully every weekend and all he sees is me worse than the last visit. I try to look excited, and act positive and hopeful when he comes to visit, but it's so obvious how I'm really doing. Just take a look at me.

"And poor Carolyn...she spends so much time with me here, watching me regress, and there's nothing she can do to fix me.

"And my other kids at home too...

"Staying alive is hard on everybody."

I decided to prepare for my death. Maybe I was fighting it and shouldn't anymore. After all, "There is a time for everything...a time to be born and a time to die..." (3)

I guess I expected a feeling, a gut feeling, that this was the end. But I didn't. A verse from the Bible came to mind. "As the heavens are higher than the earth, so are my ways higher than your ways and my thoughts than your thoughts." (4)

Thinking about that verse helped me accept my circumstances. I realized I had no control over the way things were turning out. And yet other times I was surprised, still wondering if this actually was my reality. Maybe my medications embellished my thinking, but my circumstances continually reminded me of the truth.

I wasn't scared or worried about dying; I just had some things I needed to do. That week, I wrote a letter to each of my children, and one to Al and my brother, Rob.

Now, I felt ready to die, but couldn't with this feeling of being abandoned. I became consumed with not wanting to die alone, away from my family. I needed them now more than ever. I didn't want to wait for weekends to be with them. What if I died before the next weekend even came? As I thought about it I felt an urgency to go home.

"Why hadn't the conversation of dying ever come up, especially with the fellows, or with Doctor Smith?" I wondered. "If anyone, they knew my condition the best...maybe no one wanted to discuss it."

I needed to talk to Doctor Smith right away.

I talked to a nurse about my thoughts first. She hastily told Doctor Smith and then returned to tell me that he was coming to see me.

Good. I had some concerns to discuss with him.

Carolyn was staying at Grandma's house at the time. I made sure she was out when Doctor Smith came.

My concerns spilled out. "How long are you planning to continue this medication plan? It's not working and I can't live like this anymore... I don't want to be kept alive, just so I can live longer, in a hospital, with chronic pain and suffering, slowly dying. Look at me. This isn't living anymore"

I wasn't going to beat around the bush. "And I'm here all by myself, while my family is in Penticton. It's time for me to go home so I can be with my family until I pass on."

Doctor Smith listened and understood what I was saying. He was aware of my suffering, my critical condition, and wanted to respect my wishes and decisions. But he also wanted me to know that he wouldn't ever give up hope. "I've seen worse," were specific words I heard him say. He would continue to do whatever he could to get me through this.

I told my brother, Rob, I had a meeting with Doctor Smith. Rob wanted to talk to him too. He felt frustrated and helpless. He had questions to ask and wanted answers. So Doctor Smith and Rob met with me in my room the next day.

"Why isn't my sister improving? Do you have another plan? What can I do? What can anyone do? Is there anything else that can be done?"

Looking back, it was all a bit fuzzy to me as I tried to understand what Doctor Smith said to us that day. I remember bits and pieces of him talking about Hospice in Penticton and me wanting to go home to be with my family.

Rob remembers Doctor Smith telling him that my body wasn't responding to the medication, that they had no other plan; they were doing all they could. If my condition didn't change in the next week or so, I wanted to go home. I would be put on intravenous for comfort purposes and be brought home to Penticton to spend the last part of my life with my family.

I remember the shocked look on Rob's face as Doctor Smith talked with us. Rob didn't want to hear that kind of news from

Doctor Smith. And Rob certainly didn't want me to hear it! What kind of hope would that give me?

Rob left, remembering some urgent phone calls Doctor Smith suggested he make to my parents and siblings.

When Carolyn returned she came onto my bed with me. She knew my situation was dire. "I had a talk with Doctor Smith," I started. "I'm not getting better. There isn't anything else they can do for me."

I saw her tears. She knew. We quietly cried, hung onto each other, and shared few words.

When my husband came to visit me on the weekend, I told him as he lay on my bed with me. "Al, you see how sick I am, how my body is deteriorating. You know nothing is working. I'm going to die." There, I said it.

And then I continued. "You've done so much for me; everything you could. I'm sorry, so sorry it's ending this way."

As I saw tears stream down his face, I knew I had said enough.

Another short visit and Al had to go back home; more bad news to dwell on in his head as he drove the five hour trip home. It must have been an especially long drive this time. And back to work, (the bread had to be delivered), leaving me alone again in the hospital in Vancouver.

I told my friend Baerg too. I needed to talk it out some more; she listened. That was what I needed. No big shock or surprise, or encouraging me to keep going; just ears to listen.

It had been a very difficult week. I had faced the truth of my circumstances, and awkwardly and openly shared it with those around me. I was physically and emotionally exhausted from it all.

I was often sleep deprived as the steroids I was on made it difficult for me to sleep long intervals. I would wake up about two or three times in the night and sometimes be awake for a few hours at a time. Often four or five hours were a good sleep for me.

I also made a lot of noises; grunting and groaning, in my sleep or when resting; my body's way of coping with the hard work of living. Even getting into a comfortable position while lying in bed was almost impossible. I would struggle and struggle trying to move, if only a few inches, imagining that little shuffle over would make all the difference. I would often give up the effort because it would wear me out.

"If someone could just move me a bit, just a little push, over...," I wished. What would I need help with next?

Eventually I would fall asleep in the position that I was stuck in.

Then I was taught a handy trick. If I put my arms straight above my head, I could roll myself over on the bed, adjusting myself until I was comfortable. It felt so good! With a smile of contentment on my face, I'd close my eyes, take a few deep breaths, and fall asleep.

But then I'd wake up a couple of hours later; wide awake. I would reach for the button on my bed railing that put me in a sitting position and press the "on" button for my light. I had many delusions at night. These strange dreams and thoughts seemed so meaningful and significant in the moment. I'd get my journal and pen; always in arm's reach, and start frantically writing the important details, not wanting to forget any. Occasionally when reading my journal the next morning I would cross out what I had written in the night because it didn't make sense.

But most of the time I took my delusions very seriously and often shared them with my family; trying to make sense of them as I explained in detail.

My family would roll their eyes and say to each other, "Mom's had another one of her weird hallucinations again."

A couple of days after my visit with Rob and Doctor Smith, I woke up in the middle of the night panicking and extremely anxious.

"There's not enough Ativan in the world that can help me!" I believed in my delirious state. My body vibrated and wouldn't settle down, no matter how I tried.

"What should I do? What should I do?" my mind raced. The first person that came to mind was Al... It was about 1:30 a.m.; the time he gets up for work.

"I'll call him on my cell phone," and did.

Unable to think past myself or of the impact my message would have on him I blurted out. "I'm dying, Al; all by myself in Vancouver. Help me. I'm sorry...I don't know what to do..." Caught up in my hysteria and with nothing else to say, I abruptly hung up.

But my outburst to Al didn't calm me and my madness continued. "Now what should I do?" I immediately thought of my brother and called him too.

"Hi Rob." I was still rattled. "I need you to come see me right now!"

"I'm coming right away."

"He said he was coming right away. Hurry." I repeated over and over to myself.

"I could wait for him...I'll be OK," I convinced myself...and started to settle down.

When Rob arrived, I gathered up my light, fluffy blanket.

"We'll go to the lounge," I whispered; and led the way. I didn't want us to wake up my roommate.

We sat on the couch together with my blanket wrapped around me. I was cold.

I needed to talk, "I can't do this anymore. The GVHD and the medications are killing me. You don't know how hard this is, or how weak I am," my faint voice, strained, my body shaking.

I leaned into his chest. I wanted him to share in my suffering; feel my frail body trembling against his and my skinny arms and legs as he held me.

Especially as bitter thoughts of Rob and Violet's recent traveling opportunities, (some much needed freedom and respite after spending a long season looking after her mother), bombarded me. "Do you really know how difficult it is for me...? You're having too much fun, traveling around everywhere, while I'm here suffering!"

"And don't offer me a dumb cliché for advice." I barked in my head. (He did once.)

But he didn't. Instead, he held me; my frail, broken, limp, weak, shivering body in his arms.

He talked; he tried to encourage me to push on, that I was strong and could make it through, how it was worth it to keep going, how he believed I was a fighter and shouldn't give up.

But I wasn't convinced of his inspiring words and reminded him of my reality. "I'm dying, Rob. I'm not getting better. I get older and weaker every day. Nothing is working."

He knew I was right, but couldn't let our conversation end that way. (He later told me he wished I would never look in the mirror; it would make anyone lose all hope.)

So he tried harder; kept talking, and decided he would stay as long as he needed to, even if it was the middle of the night.

We stayed in the lounge for a couple of hours. I don't remember all what he said as my mind drifted in and out, but the continuous soft monotone of his voice and his warm embrace calmed me. My body started to relax. I stopped trembling and my anxiousness went away.

I felt my countenance change; I could go on for a bit more, take on another day; a glimmer of hope; just a little, but enough.

"I'm tired." I realized; and relished in the thought of sleeping. "I want to go back to my room now."

Rob helped me up and gently and slowly walked me to my room.

"You can call me again anytime in the night if you need me and I will come. Anytime."

I knew he meant it. I slept through the rest of the night.

The next morning Rob called and said he phoned our Uncle Paul and arranged for him to come and pray with us that afternoon. He is a retired pastor and Rob felt we needed his help. Uncle Paul and his wife Auntie Anne had connected with me many times while I was in Vancouver: visited, texted, phoned, and kept me in their prayers.

Although I was looking forward to the day ahead I reflected on the past night and began to feel anxious again. My panic rose and I feared I would lose control of myself. "I need help." I worried. "How can I get help?"

Birgit, a friend I had connected with while in Vancouver, texted me; spur of the moment. She was coming into the City from Abbotsford to visit her brother and stopped by to see me as well.

She immediately sensed my anxiousness and pulled her chair close up where I lay on my bed facing her. She held my hand and listened to me, looking intensely into my eyes. Ever so gently, she quietly responded with kind and wise words. I listened intently, recognizing the guidance I was receiving that I desperately needed in that moment. I felt myself settle, my body began to relax again. Then she left; a timely and purposeful visit.

Besides Birgit, Carolyn was the first to arrive late that morning. She was never in a hurry to get to the hospital; she knew she would probably be staying late into the evening. My cousin Annette had texted me earlier that week and planned to spend the day with me. Rob, Uncle Paul, and Auntie Anne arrived in the afternoon. I sensed Jesus in my room too.

Although my company didn't all know each other, I realized we had a special connection to each other because they all came together for one reason; for me.

Let's hold hands around Marge for our prayer," Uncle Paul started.

They did; everyone stood around my bed. I pressed the button that put me in a sitting position. Uncle Paul prayed over me; everyone listened; engaged and agreeing...

It was an amazing day for me; a divine Presence lingered inside me long after everyone left. Falling asleep came easy that night.

At about 1:00 a.m., I awoke from a giant, but gentle, full-body, slow-motion hiccup; (my best effort in describing the mystifying and sensational experience.) It was fleeting, but nevertheless felt supernatural. At that same moment, in my mind, I saw something that looked like a small chunk of tofu; a white, rubbery, jelly texture. It was in the shape of a cube, about an inch long. A large, strong, but gentle hand appeared on my left side close to my rib from where the hand had removed the piece of tofu. Then I heard, "Enough suffering".

I opened my eyes as I lay there, convinced that was God's hand. And was that His voice?

I lay frozen, on my back, my eyes wide open, recalling the moment. What just happened? I knew something did. But instead of panic and anxiety, my body relaxed and I felt peace and joy on me.

Shortly after I fell back to sleep. In the morning I wrote about it in my journal and couldn't wait to tell Carolyn.

She was excited and also had a special experience that night; she'd tell me later.

I called Al to tell him my good news experience. I was grateful that he believed me and shared my excitement too!

Rob responded the same way. In fact, he thought maybe the tofu was a sign. "It means something. Maybe I should make you a dish with tofu in it. Tofu fries?" he suggested.

Yuk. That sounded awful; but I liked his enthusiasm!

Maybe we were all a little bit crazy to believe me, or just in desperate need for some good news.

I wondered, "Was it just something I conjured up, being so sick, and drugged up? Maybe it was another one of my weird hallucinations; side effects of my medication. Or maybe it was real. A miracle?"

I didn't know what to think, but I will never forget the experience: the feeling of the hiccup, seeing the hand taking the tofu thing out of my side, the words, and the peace and joy that came over me.

That night I wrote in my journal, "Every day that I am given breath, I will choose life and live." I felt a new hope inside me.

Then Carolyn told me her special experience. "I saw you last night, Mom, just like you looked before your transplant. I went over to give you a hug. When we hugged I felt strength in your body; like you used to have." They were more, much needed positive words.

However, other than a few people, I kept my experience quiet for a while, just in case... "What if no one believed my craziness... especially if my bowels didn't change?"

I felt anxious each time I went to the bathroom; wanting so badly to believe and see that my bowels improved.

"Don't play tricks on me. This isn't a joke. I need the miracle in the worst way." I kept reminding the Man upstairs.

It was a one-way conversation I had every time prior to getting myself off the toilet; and then slowly turning to peer into it...

My parents and siblings responded immediately to my brother's phone calls. They stopped everything, made spur of the moment arrangements, and arrived in my hospital room all on the same day. I didn't know how or why they all came together, but I knew it was a big trek for them. They came from all directions, traveling many miles. My dad, especially, felt a sense of helplessness. The distance between my parents and I, and their health issues prevented them from physically being a part of my journey.

Although my appearance may have initially shocked them, seeing my parents and siblings face to face was what I needed. Their presence lifted my spirit. Immediately, I felt a precious bond and connection with them; they were my blood; my family.

I noticed how my parents had aged in the last six months. I knew my illness had been very difficult for them. I saw my dad leaned over on his cane by my window; heavy breaths, (just walking from their vehicle through the hospital and into my room depleted his energy). I saw him looking at me; he noticed my frailty. His eyes were watering, but he held back the tears.

My dear mom looked confused; she didn't understand what was going on, or know who I was. (She suffers from dementia.)

My sisters each took a turn sitting on my bed with me, holding my hand, and snuggling close with me. They came to love, comfort, and support their youngest sister. There were tears, small outbursts of laughter, and quiet moments. I had been traveling a difficult journey, and they came to join and help me with my heavy load.

It was a surreal family reunion that I pondered in my heart.

My brother Rob, (donor), and me

Modeling my wig pre-transplant

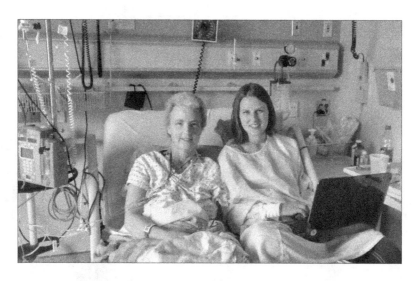

Carolyn and me watching cooking shows

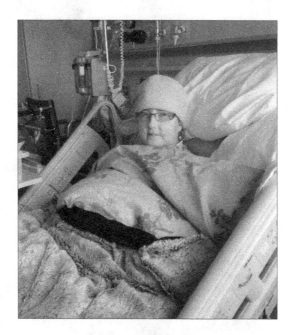

Always cold

Grandma's house

A true bride in Violet's wedding dress

Al, Zach and me — Pacific Spirit Park

Jay, Chelsey, Shaggy, and me

Carolyn, Shaggy, Neenee and me — Steveston Village

Carolyn and me

Levi, Danielle and me — Stanley Park

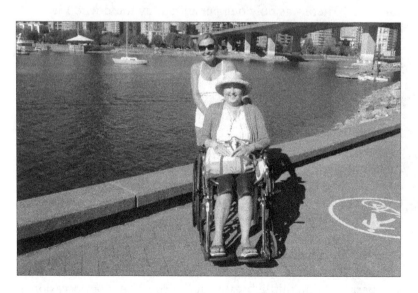

Violet and me — False Creek

13

BACK TO GRANDMA'S HOUSE WITH JOY

MY BOWELS WERE IMPROVING DAY after day and each day I was grateful for the miracle.

Because of my sudden improvement, I knew I would be discharged back to Grandma's house shortly. (I always felt the hospital's urgency for an available bed; when one patient improved, he or she was immediately discharged so one worse off and waiting, could be admitted.) There was only one person on my mind who I wanted looking after me and I was adamant about it.

"You have to look after me. You're the only one I think of. Please come.." I pleaded to my sister, Joy.

She didn't need convincing though; she was thinking the same.

I didn't know how long she could stay or how long I needed her. She didn't know either.

We hadn't spent much time together after she moved to Alberta about thirty years ago, so we had lots to catch up on; just Joy and I. She had gone through some incredible hardships that I knew little about and now was struggling with her own unique illness as well. We spent many hours talking, crying, laughing, praying, and reading devotionals together, both wanting complete healing for ourselves and for each other.

Joy found multiple tasks to do at Grandma's house, every day. Besides taking little breaks on the couch, and an occasional nap, she worked her little butt off. (Hmm, maybe that's why her butt's so small.) She cooked delicious meals for me, did the dishes, made strawberry and raspberry jam, (orders from me), washed and ironed my clothes, (I rarely iron), changed and washed my bedding every week, (I never do it weekly), did the shopping, gave me the push up the stairs that I always needed to get into the house, carried my walker down the stairs and lifted it into her car, drove me back and forth to the hospital for my appointments, cleaned the oven, scrubbed the floors, washed the carpets, dusted the furniture, washed the window sills, watered the lawn every day, (it was a dry summer in Vancouver), and did all kinds of other tasks. Oh yeah, she also painted the bathroom, living, and dining room walls, and rearranged all the furniture!

Although I was back at Grandma's house, I spent long days at the hospital, three days a week, continually receiving blood products; often six to eight hours each visit. I always cheered when Joy arrived to pick me up. I'd climb into her big, fancy truck, ride back to Grandma's house for a delicious home cooked meal, and see what projects she had worked on while I was gone. She probably should have been taking it easy, catching up on her rest, while her bossy, irritating, and demanding sister was out of her hair at the hospital. But she took her breaks when Al arrived on the weekends and happily passed me onto him.

"Yay, some respite." I figured she'd say to herself.

When requesting outings from my care givers, I often hesitated, but only momentarily. (My self-centeredness always prevailed.) I knew that it was not an easy task, hauling my wheelchair up and down stairs, in and out of the vehicle, pushing me in my wheelchair, and listening to me, a bossy passenger. But when Al came I would never give it a second thought, and took full advantage of his willingness, energy, and strength.

He often pushed me through Pacific Spirit Park in my wheelchair. It became one of our weekend routines that I always looked forward to. It was just a few blocks from the Dunbar Village strip of amenities. My wheelchair negotiated well on the wide path of mostly dirt mixed with fine gravel. On both sides of the path were tall, coniferous, evergreen trees. When you looked up towards the sky, the high reaching trees branched out at the top as an umbrella, way up there, making a tall arch over the pathway, bright and dark shades of green with small bits of blue sky beyond. There were only a few sunny spots where the sun could peek its way through. The overgrown ferns and lush ground cover blanketed the earth and climbed up the tree trunks. The air was fresh and clean, always cool on the hottest summer days. We never tired of those walks through the woods. The beauty of nature surrounded us from all around.

Once, on a rainy day, Al and I ventured out to Oakridge Mall. Our first stop where ever we went was Tim Horton's; a destination always for Al. He enjoyed his routine coffees and so we headed to the food court. (Al could spot a Tim Horton's anywhere.) As we waited in the long line for his coffee, I noticed a KFC not far away, and immediately craved chicken wings. My eyes followed a pre-planned path, past tables and chairs, other line ups, and wide enough for my wheelchair. With Al unaware and I determined to get chicken wings, I was off; slowly meandering my way through my planned path. I was amazed that I could wheel my chair, pushing the wheels forward with all the arms' strength I had. And I was pleased at how people moved out of my way accommodating the handicapped person that I was.

"Could I please have two chicken wings...no...they have to be wings...and that's everything." I requested as politely as my mad craving and mental state allowed me to.

I found a table for Al and me, and continued my journey there, settling in, excited to devour my chicken wings. I looked up to proudly wave Al over to our table.

Our conversation was about me and of how independent I was.

14

THE WEDDING DRESS

MY BROTHER, ROB, MARRIED VIOLET just short of his 50th birthday. I always admired Violet's wedding dress. It was a classic and I thought she looked gorgeous in it. The closet in my room at Grandma's house had a long zipped bag hanging in it and I suspected it was Violet's wedding dress.

I was getting more acquainted with Violet during my time in Vancouver and I noticed how very particular and careful she was with her mother's home decor. Her mother had a lot of pictures on the walls, fancy ornaments and dishes, many that they had brought over from Hungary. Everything seemed to have a designated place in the house, but every once in a while Violet would move a picture or ornament to where she thought it was more suited. She always seemed to know where everything was, and if it was moved, so I tried my best to keep things just as they were.

One Sunday afternoon after Al left for home, I headed back to my room. As I entered, I noticed the closet door was slightly opened and there was that long, zipped bag hanging...

My curiosity got the best of me. I had an idea as I sat up on my bed.

"Hey, Joy," I called out from my room.

I heard a big sigh. (She was used to constant requests.)

"Yeah, Babe?" (her affectionate name for me.) "What do you need?" her patience continually tested as she entered my room.

"Do you remember Violet's wedding dress? I think it's hanging in that zipped up bag in my closet. It's beautiful! I've always loved it." I was getting excited and bossy. "Take it out. I'll show you!"

Joy carefully took it out of the bag. It looked just like I remembered. It was taupe in color and made of satin material. The bodice was strapless with some dainty lace and beadwork, and had a matching little jacket...

Before you could say "Jack Robinson", I was wearing Violet's wedding dress! The bodice didn't quite fit my funny shape so I used one big rubber band from my bookkeeping basket and pulled it down over my head to help hold everything in the right places. From the waist down, it was the same satin material, but without the lace or beadwork and flowed beautifully to the floor. I added a straw sun hat to cover up my short, curly/frizzy, grey hair and wore my crystal, heart-shaped dangly earrings to finish it off. Unfortunately, you could see a big bandaged patch near my neck with a tube coming out, and the string around my neck that helped protect my Hickman line from being pulled out. But the tube and string both subtly tucked nicely inside the bodice. I still had dark, purple bruising on my chest, arms, and hands that could be noticed close up, a puffy face, and a distorted body, but other than that, I looked like a true bride!

I posed for Joy as she took some pictures, some of me standing and some sitting in the queen chair in the corner of my room. It was hard not to laugh. (Laughing was actually scary for me. I feared my body wouldn't be able to handle it. I had a new understanding of the expression, "die laughing".)

By the time I undressed, I was completely exhausted. But, before I lay down I made sure Joy put the dress back in the bag and hung it in the closet just as it was before. Violet would never notice! Then I settled down for a good nap; a Sunday afternoon to remember.

15

MORE NEEDLES AND A VERY BLOODY NOSE

I WAS STILL ON HIGH doses of prednisone at this time and it started to affect my blood sugar. The diabetic doctor came to see me during one of my appointments at the hospital.

"The medications that you are taking are causing your blood sugar levels to increase. You will have to start monitoring them, which involves pricking your finger several times a day and then administering insulin to yourself morning and evening..." He explained all the details.

I was grateful to have Joy listening in on the instructions. The procedure was completely foreign to me and overwhelming at the time. I had to find a different spot on my tummy area each time I injected the insulin. It added to the many already purple spots.

It was also one more thing I needed to take care of on top of everything else! I wondered if my lifestyle that required so much attention from me, my care givers, doctors, and nurses would ever end.

All this stuff to do to look after myself made me wonder. "Would I ever live a normal life where I could be independent again, look after myself without the help of others? Would I ever return to work, or fill the role of a typical mom and wife?" Keeping me alive was all consuming!

And then I developed another complication. Because my Hickman line had been inserted for quite some time, I developed a small blood clot. The doctors were concerned because it could dislodge, travel to my lungs, and possibly impede my breathing. The team decided that I needed to get rid of the clot using blood thinner medication called Dalteparin. It was injected into my stomach fat by a needle; another poke into my tummy. I had an appointment with the thrombosis doctor who gave me instructions on how to administer the medication. Thankfully, Joy accompanied me again and listened in on all the instructions I was given. The thrombosis doctor demonstrated how to inject the blood thinner and then I practiced as well.

It didn't make any sense to me though. I tried to get the fellow and thrombosis doctor to understand my perspective. "I get bags of platelets, (blood clotting cells), two or three times a week because my blood is so thin. I have purple blotches all over my body to prove it." I kept on, "Whenever I inject insulin into my stomach for my diabetes, I have to put a bandage on the sight to stop the bleeding; my blood is already way too thin. Why are you putting me on blood thinners?"

They didn't agree. They thought it was too much of a risk to ignore that small blood clot and I needed the Dalteparin to get rid of it. They assured me the fellow would monitor and, if necessary, adjust the blood thinner medication each time I visited the hospital.

Aaaaagh! I was so frustrated. I had been to the hospital every day that week for one reason or another.

I got all riled up over my circumstances again, "I do enough poking every day. There is no end to what they add to my medical problems. What will they find out and come up with next? Maybe I should stay away from the hospital. Then they wouldn't be able to find things wrong with me. I don't even want to know what's wrong anymore. Stop looking so hard. Maybe then all my problems would go away. Isn't there a slogan, 'Ignorance is bliss'?"

It's hard to win when dealing with a specialist and fellow from hematology, so I gave in with a big sigh, and picked up three boxes of Dalteparin blood thinner injection needles from the pharmacy. I started to give myself a daily injection at dinner time.

I got a nose bleed the second night after taking the injection. I woke up from swallowing. It took a few moments for me to realize I was swallowing blood. But it went away after a couple of minutes and I fell back to sleep.

The next night it happened again. When I awoke, I recognized what it was immediately. I lay still, on my back, and swallowed the blood, assuming it would stop like the night before, but it got worse, trickling out of my nose as well. I sat up and pinched my nose to stop the bleeding, but blood kept coming out no matter how tight I pinched. At the same time, I kept swallowing blood that was dripping down the back of my throat.

Joy woke up right away. She always heard me when I got up, grunted or wrestled around in my bed and would say, "Are you OK, Babe?"

She came in right away, saw the bleeding, and got me some toweling. While I was pinching my nose shut, I phoned the nurse on call at the hospital. She told me to sit up, bend my head forward, and pinch my nose tight until the bleeding stopped. But it didn't.

After about fifteen minutes I started to panic. My mind raced, "What do I do? What do I do? I can't stay here and keep bleeding like this. I have to get up, get out of bed. I can't get out of bed. I'll have to get to the hospital, but how? I can't. It's too hard for me. I have to keep holding my nose. There's so much blood! I'm tired, so frail, and in my P.J.s! It's 4:00 in the morning. How will I do this? Why is this happening?"

I called the nurse back to let her know that my nose wouldn't stop bleeding. She told me to come to Emergency right away and the doctor would be notified. I knew I was losing a lot of blood and now I had to get myself to the hospital in the middle of the night.

My panic continued to rise. "This is so hard. How will I get myself in Joy's truck? I have to keep pinching my nose. Why doesn't the bleeding stop? Will Joy be OK? She must be so tired. But she has to help me! I can't do this. When will this craziness stop? Is this still that dumb dream?"

Trying to get myself out of bed with one hand pinching my nose was awkward. My other hand used the bed rail to pull me up. I couldn't get my Alpaca socks on so I wiggled my fat feet into the sandals that I kept on the floor right next to my bed. I kept swallowing blood, trying to keep my head down, while pinching my nose. My eyes hurt from trying to look up so I could see where I was going. I better get to the bathroom first...still awkward; getting on the toilet...and all the other details. This is so hard.

I got myself to the front door and looked into the darkness towards the truck. "Can I even do this?" I wondered as my energy already felt depleted. I hadn't gone outside the house in the dark before. It seemed extra dark.

The effort needed to focus seemed overwhelming. So I yelled orders in my head, "Don't fall. Hang on to the rail, tight. I can't see. Lift your feet high...don't trip. The truck is so far away. This is awful!"

...more panic, stress, shaking.

Then a Presence came over me and in my mind I heard the words "Don't panic. It's going to be OK."

Immediately calmness came over me. I felt my body relax, and the effort and ability required to focus suddenly seemed easier.

I gingerly negotiated the stairs; talking quietly and slowly to myself, "Careful on the steps...one foot in front of the other... you're on the sidewalk. Lift your feet with every step...don't trip. Keep going...keep your head down...pinch tighter! ...you're almost at the truck."

Joy had the door open for me.

I kept talking to myself, "Grab the handle and pull yourself in. OK, good...you did it!"

Joy already had lots of tissue and a rag for me when I got in my seat. I focused on holding my head down and pinching my nose. I continued to swallow blood while at the same time it trickled into the rag I held in front of my nose.

The Emergency room was quiet when I arrived and was immediately directed to an available bed. I was given some nose pinchers right away. My fingers were stiff and sore when I let go of my nose. I hadn't realized how tight I was pinching. I was hooked up to a machine that tracked my vitals and given a bag of platelets. I continued to swallow blood for about another two hours before I noticed the constant trickling in the back of my throat slow. Joy went back home to get some sleep. I'm not sure if she slept, but she came back with everything I needed: some food, my phone, my medication, and a change of clothes for going home. I was so thankful for her care and reminded of how dependent I was. What would I have done without her?

The doctor came in later that morning to see how I was doing and said I could go home around noon. But I was aghast when he told me to take my blood thinner medication at dinner time!

Adamantly and flailing my arms in desperation to be listened to with a plug on my nose, I argued back. "No! I'm not taking that needle tonight. I just went through a horrifying night! I am not going through that again!"

MORE NEEDLES AND A VERY BLOODY NOSE

"Why wouldn't anyone listen to me?" I wondered. I felt like I was fighting for my life.

"Why do you give me blood thinners when I need platelets every other day? I've had this nose plug on for six hours." I could feel my water ballooned neck jiggling as I disputed.

For a moment, I imagined being in his shoes, and wondered if he would listen to, and take this crazy-looking, hysterical, and plug-on-her-nose lady seriously.

The moment ended quickly though; I was too concerned with my wellbeing. It had been a dreadful night and I didn't want it repeated.

Looking at me bewildered, he responded, "I'll come back and discuss it with you again before you're discharged."

As soon as he left I threw my hands over my face and cried out in panic, "God, no! You have to be my advocate! I can't take that blood thinner tonight. Please change his mind. I need Your help. Help me!" I felt so desperate.

As soon as the doctor returned I started again; desperately pleading and repeating myself. "I can't take that blood thinner tonight!"

He interrupted, "Leave the blood thinner for tonight; your fellow will advise you tomorrow when you go for your treatment."

"Thank you," I replied humbly; to the doctor and to God.

Joy picked me up and we went back to Grandma's house. That was the end of my blood thinner injections. I wondered if the fellows forgot about it; they never mentioned or prescribed it to me again; I didn't remind them either.

Much later, I happily donated the three boxes of Dalteparin back to the hospital.

The day after my bleeding nose incident, I was sent to an ear, nose, and throat specialist. He gave me instructions on how to prevent further bleeding. Using a wooden popsicle stick type applicator, he took a small glob of Vaseline and applied it to the inside of both of my nostrils. I watched carefully and asked detailed questions of a very simple procedure, hoping that my careful and best effort could prevent another nose bleed like I had just experienced.

I wanted the same applicator as he used, but couldn't find one at the drugstore in Dunbar Village where Joy and I shopped.

"Q-tips will probably work just fine," Joy offered.

"No, they won't!" I protested. "It has to be like what he used..."

But we couldn't find anything close to the applicator he used. And so with me unaware, Joy picked up a box of Q-tips.

All that day, my mind was consumed with wanting the right applicator. I talked non-stop about my big problem to Joy.

And then finally, I had a great idea. "Joy, you know those wooden stir sticks they have at Starbucks for stirring coffee? Those will work!" I wished I could go get them myself. I imagined myself running to Starbucks right then, buying a coffee to justify grabbing a small stack of stir sticks from the self-serve counter. It would have been so easy. But I couldn't even walk.

And Joy didn't feel the same urgency that I did. How could I get her to get me what I wanted?

In the meantime, Joy had snuck the Q-tips she purchased on my bathroom counter, just in case I reconsidered.

"I told you...Q-tips won't work!" And instead I chased her all day with my unrelenting request. "You have to go to Starbucks and get me those stir sticks!"

It was an unnecessary and silly request, but she knew the issue wouldn't be put to rest until I got my way.

16

MEDICATION SIDE EFFECTS

IT WAS THE MIDDLE OF June and for three months now I had been on very high doses of prednisone along with seven or eight other medications. Some of them were anti-rejection pills, helping do a similar job to the prednisone. Others were protecting me from viruses, infections, and diseases that I was susceptible to because of my compromised immune system. Although my prednisone was slowly being tapered down again, each of these medications had different side effects and the longer I was on them, the more I struggled with some of their effects.

Because some of my medications were types of steroids, struggling with sleep was one of the side effects. Previously, I looked forward to going to my bed. Everything around my body felt soft and warm: the mattress, the pillows, and the blankets. It was all so comforting and relaxing in a peaceful, quiet room.

But then when I struggled to fall and stay asleep I dreaded night time, anxiously worrying about it, and only making matters worse. I began taking Ativan to calm me down which initially helped me fall asleep, but then I would routinely wake up an hour or two later, usually around 11:30 or midnight with severe panic attacks. It was very scary. I felt out of control, like I was falling in mid-air, or going to go crazy, and didn't know how to help myself out of it. I'd be wide awake with my mind racing, "What should I do? What should I do?" I couldn't calm myself down. I would worry about the long night ahead of me, afraid of being awake all night, panicking that I would never heal for lack of sleep. (I was continually reminded that sleep was important for my healing.) That would cause more anxiety, making it even harder to fall back to sleep.

I would pull myself up on my bed and do all kinds of things to try to distract my mind. Sometimes I would read for a bit, or text drafts that I would send later in the morning, or play Solitaire on my i-pad, listen to calming music on my i-pod, or catch up on my journal writing.

Doing the book keeping for my husband's company also helped distract my mind. I would quickly become completely focused on the task. It became an effective way to calm me down. It also made me feel useful and productive. Al would drop off a box of his paper work when he came to visit and take a box home that I had completed to be filed away. Most of the book work was repetitious so my brain remembered how to complete it. Some components that I couldn't remember how to do would have to wait. I was usually aware, sometimes with a reminder from Al, which transactions were important and had deadlines, and made sure they were completed on time.

After two or three hours, I would attempt to go back to sleep. And if I did, I would often wake up again and start over with some or all of these activities. I kept everything that I needed for the night on my bed or on the shelf of the head board so I could retrieve them without having to get up or move my body across the bed. The lap top and basket of paper work, including pencil, pen, stapler, paperclips, scissors, and elastics, as well as my journal, reading books, i-pad, i-pod, cell phone, pain, sleeping, and anti-anxiety medications, water, and tissue were all within arm's reach. Everything had its place.

Besides my mind racing, my body felt like it was racing too. My legs became overly restless. I'd have an intense urge to wiggle and move them around, but I couldn't because they were too heavy for my weak muscles.

I would often wonder, "Why do my legs feel like they each weigh a hundred pounds?!"

They would also feel prickly, uncomfortable, and sometimes like ants were crawling under my skin. The sensation felt like electricity inside me; I called it buzzing. I would wake up and find myself grunting and groaning, trying to maneuver my body into a comfortable position, but I couldn't get relief. It was exhausting; I felt like I was going to go berserk, waiting for this uncontrollable urge to pass.

MEDICATION SIDE EFFECTS

Besides anti-anxiety medication, I took sleeping pills to help settle me. It sometimes helped me back to sleep, but it was never long enough. I would wake up from the same side effects and start over again.

Joy would wake up from her light sleep, often hearing me making continuous grunting sounds. My body would squirm, twitch, and jerk in my sleep or even while I was resting. I wasn't aware of my noisy, squirmy body until I would hear her say, "Are you OK, Babe?"

I would also get panic attacks during the day. I would go to my bed where I felt comfortable, but I would feel myself losing control. Carolyn was there for a lot of my panic attacks. She would come and lie beside me, hold my hand or just snuggle with me, help me focus on slower breathing, and talk sense into me, constantly and gently reassuring me.

"What's bothering you, Mom...?

"Oh, it'll be alright...

"I can do that for you in the morning...

"You don't have to worry about that...

"I'll help you with that when you need it...

"I'll be here with you..."

She was remarkably equipped to calm me down, many, many times. I gravely relied on her to help me through those mental battles. And when she wasn't there, I learned to call on others for help.

Zach liked to come and join me on my bed. I felt delinquent as a mother; especially for Zach. He was in Grade 10 and I had spent most of the year away from him and our home. But I was helpless too; I had no ability to care for him as I wanted to.

As he lay beside me, he would remind me. "Mom, we don't expect anything from you. We just want you to get better so you can come home."

I loved hearing that. I had nothing to offer, and he had no expectations of me. His nearness and words helped relax me. Then once, I combed my fingers through his hair like I used to. He soaked up the affection; and repeatedly returned for more... Although it was such a small act of love, I realized I did have something to offer him.

Joy had done so much for me. Every day in the middle of her own pain, I pushed her to her limit, especially when I wanted to get away from the same old; Grandma's house and the hospital. I wouldn't back down until she gave in. With all the strength she had, she'd lift my wheel chair in and out of the back of her big truck, help me up and down the stairs of Grandma's house, and carry all my belongings for me. It was such an ordeal; just getting to the truck which was only about twenty feet from the front door.

Every time we stepped out, we imagined how entertaining it may have been for our senior neighbors; drawn to their windows to watch. Maybe they were thinking, "Where are those strange ladies headed today?"

They probably knew our routine of getting from the house to the truck as well as we did; and backwards when we'd return home.

Sometimes I would just want a simple walk in the fresh air in Dunbar Village. It was pleasure for me; a ride in my wheelchair. But Joy had to do all the work, pushing the wheelchair up and down the sidewalks.

"Oh, can we go here...see this...get that...?" until she was exhausted.

Because of all the medication I continued to be on, I developed high blood pressure. So I added another pill to my repertoire to help stabilize it.

Joy's task of helping me manage my ever-increasing medication variety was challenging. "Did you check your blood sugar yet? Do it now, before your meal. Did you give yourself your insulin yet? How are your numbers? Did you take your blood pressure pill?"

Keeping track of it all required constant remembering, and I wasn't able to manage everything myself.

It had been an intense month for Joy and I'm sure she was glad when her husband Alan came to take her back home; but not without a few extra day trips. It became Alan's job to push my wheelchair. He took us to Stanley Park for some chicken fingers and fries. We enjoyed a day at Granville Island, and a lovely July 1st, full moon evening at Spanish Banks where we watched the locals crabbing.

Before Joy and Alan left, Rob and Violet took us out for breakfast at their tennis club. We sat outside where the restaurant extended out over the ocean. The skies were clear; there was a gentle, warm breeze and waves lapped gently onto the sandy shore. It was a beautiful spot. This was a moment that made me feel like I was on a holiday.

We sat around the elegant table setting enjoying a delicious breakfast, as well as a fun conversation. I looked over at Violet thinking it was the right time to share the wedding dress story with her.

"Violet, I have to tell you a story. It's about your wedding dress...!"

I immediately caught her attention; and Joy's...as she glanced over at me, her eyes a bit wider than usual. I knew what she was thinking, "Are you kidding?!"

It was too late to back down. Being seated in my wheelchair at the head of the table, I immediately felt everyone's attention on me. They all seemed to lean in a bit as I shared the story.

Everyone was well entertained; especially at the end when I remembered that I had photos to share from my cell phone to accompany the story.

My time with Joy came to an end. I wasn't sure how I would survive without her. I had become so used to her taking care of me. We had gotten to know each other again, after a very long time, sharing so much of ourselves with each other. I loved every minute I spent with her.

17

AT GRANDMA'S HOUSE WITH NEENEE

AS JOY AND ALAN LEFT back for Alberta, Al arrived for his regular short weekend visit. As he left, my oldest sister Neenee arrived at Grandma's house. She came restocking the kitchen with a cooler full of salmon, halibut and other goodies. Neenee proved to be another excellent cook and I looked forward to every breakfast, lunch and dinner. Despite the pain she battled through, from a complicated knee replacement, her focus was on me. I felt very safe and secure with her. She treated me like I was her little girl; helpless and struggling as I was. She played a loving motherly role; doing all she could to help me in my illness. I often noticed her face wince in pain, especially when she struggled to carry my wheelchair up and down the stairs, or lift it in and out of her SUV.

We enjoyed planning meals together. Even my bagged lunch for my hospital day became gourmet! I would have four or five little containers of this and that; something to look forward to during my long day at the hospital.

We also planned day trips when I wasn't heading to the hospital.

"Let's go shopping at Oakridge Mall and maybe we can make a trip to Steveston Village this week," Neenee offered.

We did both. I was thrilled for the day trips. We enjoyed shopping one day, and my daughter and niece, Shaggy, joined us for a beautiful, sunny afternoon at Steveston Village; another holiday feeling.

Neenee always encouraged me to have company over whenever possible. Maybe it meant a bit of respite for her, but she also knew it was important for me and something I looked forward to. So we arranged for my sister-in-law, Heather, niece, Shaggy, and nephew, William, to come for dinner.

"What can we bring?" Heather offered.

I already had dinner preplanned in my head. "You can bring a roasted chicken and we, (I meant, Neenee), will do the rest."

I was very excited about our dinner plans. Although I was still on a low fibre diet, I would allow myself to eat the crispy skin and crunch on the small bones of the chicken wings. Neenee was preparing the rest of dinner while I imagined, (excitement rising in me), our delicious dinner.

I was getting impatient and texted Heather, "Where are you?"

She texted back to tell me they were almost at Grandma's house, but picked up some fish instead. The deli department they stopped at was out of roasted chickens.

My cantankerous behavior suddenly took over and I immediately phoned her. "Heather, we can't have fish. I've planned on chicken."

There was silence. William had been driving across the City in busy Saturday afternoon traffic, stopping at busy grocery parking lots and crowded stores to find a roasted chicken. It was not a simple request and I knew it.

But I broke the awkward silence and continued on with my bossy behavior. "You can put the fish in our fridge when you get here and take it home with you. We have to have chicken! Pick one up here at Stongs. They never run out."

I was set on chicken wings and it wasn't in me to have it any other way.

But why was I unable to back down on something so trivial? I liked fish too. Maybe it was because I had so little control of my life that any little bit I thought I could demand from others, (especially those closest to me), I did. Or maybe medication that I continued to be on was still partly the cause of my crotchety behavior. Plus Prednisone was known to increase one's appetite, and my craving for specific foods was often intense causing hunger pangs. Whatever the reason and most likely a combination of them all, I continually, but regretfully confirmed my nickname, "Marge, the Sarge," (sergeant).

A couple of days later, two of my cousins, Eunice and Karen, came to visit. They looked forward to their planned day trip as much as I appreciated them coming; Eunice left from the little town of Yarrow, and picked up Karen along the way. Neenee and our cousins visited with me in my room; I had little strength that day and needed the comfort of my bed. As the day progressed, I was periodically distracted with my wellbeing; something wasn't right. The mirror of the dresser on the opposite wall faced me as I sat up on my bed. I looked at myself occasionally. My face looked pale...

But, then I would engage back into the conversation, enjoying everyone in my room, and ignoring my physical symptoms; hoping it wasn't anything concerning.

After they left, I went to the bathroom. I was in the habit of always checking what went into the toilet. Oh no! There was a huge volume of blood; and later, again. I called the hospital and was readmitted back on the fifteenth floor of the Jim Pattison Pavilion. Neenee left for home the next day. It was the second week in July.

18

VERY BAD BLEEDING

MORE BLOOD TRANSFUSIONS: PLATELETS AND hemoglobin; at least one or the other every day. My prednisone was brought back up to maximum doses and yet my blood counts continued to drop. My low hemoglobin counts made me very fatigued and discouragement followed closely behind. How would I ever be able to leave this place if my body was always losing so much blood? I needed another miracle.

It was a serious matter as the team struggled to figure out the source of my bleeding. The fellow had a gastroscopy arranged for me. A camera on the end of a scope is put down your throat and wiggled down as far as it can go in order to locate the bleeding. I was well sedated and didn't feel or remember anything; relieved that it was so easy.

But unfortunately, they didn't find the bleeding location, so the next step was a colonoscopy. I dreaded the procedure as it was explained to me. This time the camera goes up your rectum and is wiggled up as far as they can get it; through your large and then small intestines. Just prior to the procedure you have to drink two liters of a solution that cleans out your intestines shortly after consumption. That is a lot of liquid to drink, especially for someone who is already bloated from fluid retention.

I didn't think the pre colonoscopy solution drink was even necessary. My bowels were always working overtime and I was sure my intestines were cleaned out enough. However, it's hard to argue with protocol.

Fortunately, my nurse displayed extra compassion towards me. "You drank enough." He said as he noticed about a half liter left on my bed table.

"Thanks." It felt like the solution had filled me up to the back of my throat and was going to overflow into my mouth if I drank anymore.

Unfortunately, things only got worse from there on. As soon as I was transferred to a transport bed to go to the procedure room, I went into survival mode, starting with a careless porter. In most of my transporting experiences, the porters had been very good drivers, careful through doorways and keeping my IV pole close enough to me with always plenty of slack, while even carrying on a pleasant conversation. I was always able to relax on those rides.

...except for this one. As we headed through the first doorway, my bed and I took several bumps and bangs back and forth on either side of the doorway before getting through. Then my IV pole headed down the hall on its own, without the porter being aware. The IV tubing pulled at my Hickman line. I was quick to grab the line and hold some slack until I reached my destination in fear of my line being ripped out of my chest. I felt anxious, exhausted, and helpless before I even reached the procedure room.

Under normal circumstances, a colonoscopy is not much different than a gastroscopy, as far as how the patient fared. However, the medications I was currently on did not allow for the amount of pain medication needed for this particular procedure. In other words, I felt excruciating pain and cramping. I remember groaning in agony, trying to curl up in a fetal position in an effort to reduce the pain, but I had no muscle strength to move. I was partly sedated and trapped in a helpless body struggling to just endure the pain. It seemed to take forever.

When the fellow came in the next day, he explained the results. "We weren't able to get the camera far enough in; only into your large intestines. We need to get into your small intestines. We'll have to give it another try,"

I glared up at him with an ever-increasing, anxious reaction, "What? Are you kidding? I can't do that again! If you couldn't get through, why would you try again?"

"It's like taking a shot at the basketball hoop," the fellow casually responded. "If you don't make the first shot, you try again."

I hated his analogy. "I'm not doing it again."

After a couple of days I calmed down and told the fellow I would let him know when I was ready for the next colonoscopy. He understood.

But it didn't make me feel any better. Another colonoscopy; how could I endure it? How did my body keep going? Did the medical team know that I could survive another one? I certainly didn't; I was so frail and weak.

But what were my options? There was nothing I could do to stop the bleeding. My circumstances weren't improving, always changing, but never for the better. This nightmare was never ending; it just kept going on and on…bad things kept happening to me and I wasn't waking up from it.

I cried, continually. I'd pull my sheet over my head and cry quietly on my bed while I rested during the day. When a nurse or the fellow came in to talk to me, I couldn't hold back tears. I cried myself to sleep at night. Every time I woke up in the night I cried some more; there was no end to it.

"It's OK to cry." I told myself. "This is so hard…" My private and continual crying felt like the only way to comfort myself. Besides, it was too hard to stop.

The fellow noticed and was concerned. "About your crying… I'm going to have the psychiatrist come in and see you. She will be able to prescribe some anti-depressants to help you through. It's important that you keep a positive attitude."

Sudden anger flared up in me. (I didn't want my newly discovered coping mechanism threatened by more drugs!) I needed to defend myself as thoughts spun around in my head, some of them spewed out at him in words. My dignity, politeness, and control of my emotions were lost somewhere in my circumstances. "Are you crazy; anti-depressants? What do you expect? You just put me through a torturous colonoscopy and want to repeat it again. This is my body and you're treating me as though I'm just a project…experiment…well, I'm not. I feel all the pain…you don't. Have you forgotten what I've been through? Now you want to throw more drugs at me?"

I kept ranting and yelling inside my head. "I've been in and out of the hospital for four months now. Will I ever get out of here? It's like I'm stuck in a prison and I can't get out. Of course my emotions are out of control. Everything in my life is out of control. And being doped up every day with a pile of drugs doesn't help either. What's wrong with you?"

I started to dislike the hospital and everything about it. It seemed like I was caught and trapped in an institution that I had no way of getting out of.

A social worker named Darcy was assigned to me when I was first admitted onto T15. She heard I was struggling, (that's an understatement), and stopped in to see me. I ranted and raved while she sat and listened to me. She didn't have the medical knowledge, but she cared about ME. I spilled it all out; everything the fellow mentioned that I didn't want to hear about, including the psychiatrist coming in to see me, the anti-depressants, that they wanted to repeat the painful colonoscopy, and more. Darcy kept listening.

I calmed down, temporarily and apologized to the fellows and nurses. I knew I had been rude and disrespectful to every one of them.

They all responded in the same way. "It's OK, Marge. You don't need to apologize...you're going through a lot..."

They understood. They knew my journey well. They continued on their quest for my recovery, even when I continued to act up. They wouldn't give up, no matter what.

The psychiatrist came in the next day. Of course I couldn't hold back the tears when she entered my room and introduced herself. Everything and everybody made me cry.

I listened to her spiel; but I couldn't agree with her. "It's situational." I argued. "It's been a really tough week...and I'll get over it. You don't know what I've been through. You'd be crying too."

She had a way about her that made me believe she was listening to me, but no matter what I said, she wouldn't take no for an answer. I tried my best to persuade her that I would be OK without the medication, but I started to cave. I was all worn out from failing to negotiate with her. I knew Al would be coming the next day. What if I couldn't help but cry all weekend when he came to visit? Our visits were so short; I didn't want him to see me this way, life was hard enough on him without me crying all weekend. So I gave in.

I could hardly wait for Al to come. His weekly visits and emotional strength gave me renewed energy that I desperately depended on until the next weekend. Al arrived and I hardly cried at all that weekend. I didn't really even think or worry about it. But I stayed on the anti-depressant medication. Maybe it was working.

I often woke up several times in the night with an intense urge to pee. (I must have lost all pelvic muscle needed to control my bladder.) I would get myself sitting up on the edge of my bed and squeeze my behind as tight as I could...waiting...until the urge subsided enough that I felt I could get up and make it to the bathroom on time. I always made it; but not this time. As I took the first few steps to head to the bathroom, a sensation of warm liquid left my bottom.

"What?" I looked down to the floor; a pool of blood around me.

I turned back towards my bed and reached for my call bell. My nurse came in, saw the blood, and hastily helped me back to bed, calling for other nurses to help. They came immediately; six of them surrounded my bed. My nurse flicked the bright light above my bed on, exposing the bloody mess all around me.

I lay on my bed wide awake watching all the action in front of me. I could feel the anxiety and panic in the nurses. It was very frightening and concerning for them to see all the blood I had lost and not be able to stop it, or know why or where I was bleeding. My nurse called for a bag of blood and then decided to call for more bags of blood. Two other nurses began wiping up the blood on the floor heading to the bathroom while other nurses began cleaning me and my bed up. They worked efficiently and with learned skill, changing me into a clean gown and changing my bed sheets; turning me this way and that way in the process. They accomplished it quickly without me even having to get off my bed.

"How are you feeling, Marge? Everything is going to be OK," my nurse blurted out, hovered over me, nervously straightening the clean bed sheets around me.

"I'm OK," and surprisingly I was. I thought I should be panicking along with the nurses and feeling exhausted from the large volume of blood lost. But I wasn't; instead I felt energized, yet peaceful.

There was one nurse at my bedside I recognized from seeing her on the ward. I didn't know her name; she had never been assigned to take care of me. But she reminded me of someone, so I took the opportunity...

"You know who you remind me of?" I asked looking up at her as she busily helped put a soaker pad underneath my bottom in case there would be more bleeding. "You look like Velma from Scooby-Doo." I chuckled. "Do you know who she is?"

She didn't. But other nurses did; and they chuckled, catching my eye and smirking with me. The atmosphere in my room changed at that moment. The panic around me stopped, the frenzy left the room, and everyone relaxed.

I received continuous bags of blood throughout the rest of the night and the following day. My blood counts had dropped to a critical low. I was reminded and grateful I had given blood as a young adult. I was even more grateful for those who presently were giving blood for me. It was my life line.

I didn't know why or how but that was the end of my bleeding. It stopped abruptly. I was overjoyed every time there wasn't blood in the toilet. I called it my second miracle.

But the nurses and fellow didn't share my excitement. They knew the seriousness of my bleed and were more concerned about finding the location than celebrating a miracle.

I had the second painful colonoscopy that had the same results as the first.

I had a few small spots of blood after the second colonoscopy, but the fellow offered me good news. "The bit of blood may have been from the irritation of the procedure." And then he continued; to remind me, his head nodding with confusion. "We still haven't found the location of the bleeding."

"Well, I haven't had any bleeding..." I didn't share his concern.

"We still need to locate the bleeding; it's too serious to just hope it won't happen again because it most likely will," he kept pushing. "There is one other procedure...blah blah blah..."

"I'm not interested," I responded with intentional politeness. But in my head, I yelled, "Procedures, procedures...leave me alone! I'm sick of procedures!"

"I need a break from all these procedures," I continued out loud and appropriately.

Inside, I was still rejoicing that the bleeding had stopped.

After a few more days, good news came. "We're going to discharge you at the end of the week. Book appointments for Mondays, Wednesdays, and Fridays at the day clinic to receive the blood products you will require. And, we still want you to consider having one last procedure in an attempt to locate the bleeding."

I think I only heard the discharge from the hospital part of the short conversation.

19

A NEW COMPLICATION

AS PART OF MY DAILY routine at the hospital, I would take my IV pole and walk a few circles around the ward. The intention was to keep my muscles functioning as the medication worked against them. It became more difficult over time, my muscles shrinking, especially from the high doses of prednisone that was increased again because of my bleeding. It was very discouraging, but now that the bleeding had stopped, I anticipated my prednisone intake decreasing again.

However, it was difficult for the team to know what to do. If my prednisone, (sometimes referred to as the miracle drug), was reduced, there was the risk of another serious bleed. But if they kept me on such high doses, (as I had been for such a long period of time), it would continue to wreak havoc on my muscles. I was afflicted with severe atrophy. How much more could my body take before the damage became long lasting?

Although my bleeding had stopped, my body had been through such trauma, that my bone marrow was no longer producing its own blood. So, I continued to receive blood transfusions about every other day. After a bag or two of blood products, my energy level would increase and I would take my IV pole for a walk around the ward. My legs continued weakening and my IV pole became my crutch, helping support me as I slowly made my round, each time surprised at how difficult it had become. I used to practice stepping up and down on a low stepping stool but now I couldn't even do that. I used to walk four or five rounds at a time.

Now I anticipated turning the last corner and heading to my room after one round.

One morning I was routinely walking my lap around the ward. As I reached out to press the button on the wall that opened the door ahead of me, my toe nicked the base of my IV pole. I instantly collapsed to the floor. Because I was close to the wall when it happened, my body crumbled into the wall as I dropped. I cried out in pain; lying helpless on the floor against the wall.

Immediately there was a big commotion; nurses all around and more nurses rushing towards me carrying a big tarp with large straps extending from it. Hastily they spread the tarp out on to the floor next to me; teaming with each other...and then gingerly maneuvered my body onto the tarp; lifting it with me crumpled inside and onto a bed.

I was sent for x-rays that afternoon to see what damage I had incurred. I kept repeating the details of my fall in my head in slow motion, over and over, second by second, and thinking, "I didn't hear a crack...maybe hitting the wall first softened my fall to the floor, probably just a bad bruise..."

"I'm sorry to tell you...the x-ray shows a fracture in your hip. You will need surgery," the fellow explained. "I will have the surgeon come in to talk to you about it in more detail."

I couldn't stand hearing the news and battled with my thoughts, "No! How could this happen to me? Why did I do that? I didn't mean to fall. My big toe just nicked my IV pole... I had no muscles to catch my fall. Awful! Awful! This is terrible!"

I was extremely angry with myself. "Aaaagh! Just when I was going to be discharged back to Grandma's house; one step closer to going home. Now this. What a stupid thing I did. Stupid, stupid."

I didn't want to tell Al, or anybody for that matter. More bad news. I didn't even want the nurses to know what happened to me. They were always rooting for me; everyone was. And now look at what I'd done.

Thankfully, that's not what the nurse who was caring for me the next day said to me. "It was an accident... The muscles in your legs are suffering terribly from atrophy. It could have happened to anyone in your situation...don't beat yourself up about it."

I needed to hear that over and over as my thoughts went back and forth, "Of course, I didn't mean to...but it still happened. What a careless accident; but I was just trying to do the right thing; getting my exercise; but look what I did."

It was hard for me to forgive myself. And the side effects of my medications didn't help with my emotions either. I was frustrated and angry. I knew it was a big setback for me. So did everyone else.

The bruising showed immediately; just above my knee and all the way up to my waist. My leg and buttock turned dark, navy blue; almost black.

Life seemed at its worst again. I lay flat on my back waiting to hear when I could be scheduled in for surgery; maybe today, maybe tomorrow. Every day I hoped it was that day. The only position I could be was on my back. I misplaced my phone, and couldn't move to look for it. Every day seemed endless. I lay staring up at the ceiling, sometimes feeling like I would go bonkers with nothing to do. I couldn't even look forward to meal time. I was back on ice cubes only. I couldn't eat for twelve hours before surgery and they didn't know until late in the day if I would get in. By that time I missed dinner as well as breakfast and lunch. My emotions were habitually all out of whack from my circumstances and medications. Prednisone also increases your appetite; I felt like I was going mad from hunger cravings. I had been learning to live one day at a time, but now one moment at a time was stretching my ability.

In general I was very miserable. Every little thing irritated and easily provoked me. I had a male nurse one day who initially seemed pleasant and friendly, but then he constantly came to my bed side; talk, talk, talk. I couldn't stomach him after a while. I had a loud one-way conversation in my head with him as he blabbed on and on...

"Please shut up! I don't want to hear your dumb stories. You must have more important things to do...like help me find my phone. Go away!" (Maybe some of my words spewed out at him as well.) It didn't matter though; he kept coming back to yak some more.

A new patient was admitted into my room in the middle of the night. There was a whole entourage that came along, stayed, and carried on a conversation that was too loud and long for my liking at that time of night.

"Quiet! I'm trying to sleep!" I yelled. Immediately I started hurling whatever I could get my hands on at them, only to become more frustrated as my feeble muscles barely lobbed the objects past the foot of my bed. The small crowd all turned, looking bewildered at me.

I had to rely on a nurse every time nature called. The nurse would bring a bed pan and help me roll to the side as she slid it under my bottom. Then I'd have to call her back when I was done. I'd roll to the side again to expose my bottom and my bruising, as she gingerly wiped my butt, and moved the pan out from under me; sometimes awkwardly spilling the contents onto my bed...

"Why was my life like this?"

Fortunately for me, I usually had a nurse come into my room positive and upbeat, despite my pathetic behavior. I felt supported and cared for although completely undeserved. They believed in me and knew that I couldn't help being the crotchety person that I had become.

The weekend arrived which meant Al was coming to visit me and my hope for surgery wouldn't happen now until at least Monday. I would have to continue to lie on my back the entire weekend.

My emotions continued to be unpredictable, usually for the worse. Al arrived, exhausted from the long drive and focused on the chair he spotted in the corner of my room where he could plop his self into for a much needed power snooze. He was holding a box of ginger snaps that he had been snacking on. I grabbed them from his hand and started shoving them into my mouth, growling and glaring at him like an angry bear.

I viciously stared him down, spitting out ginger snaps as I ordered, "Quit just sitting around here, Al...you should be helping more...don't expect the nurses to do everything...you don't have a clue what it takes to look after me!"

Al was startled by the sudden attack.

He knew the medication was affecting my behavior, but this was too much! He stood up, momentarily looked around hoping not to see spectators, (but then didn't care), leaned in close to me, looked me straight in the eye, and said loud and clear, "Just grow up!"

"Cough, sputter...," I almost choked on my ginger snaps. (I wasn't expecting that.) But he put me in my place. It was what I needed to hear. I wasn't the only one having a hard time. My circumstances were extremely difficult for those close to me as well.

Surgery finally happened on Monday.

On Tuesday the surgeon came in to see me, "The surgery went well. We used three pins, each about four inches long to hold everything back together again. However, because of your situation, there may be some permanent damage done to some of your nerves and muscles. Keep up with your exercises and time will tell."

The physiotherapist came in everyday for the next week, giving me exercises to work on to begin the long and slow process of muscle building to walk again.

"Your doctor is ready to discharge you, that is, if you can manage the stairs...you'll need to get into your house. Are you up for it?" the physiotherapist asked on her next visit.

I didn't think I could do it, but if she thought I was ready, I'd give it a try.

She explained a specific process that made the task possible; and required my full concentration. My brain had to remember each body movement in order and then send the message to my muscles to act the motions out. Grab the railing with my arms, strong leg up on the first step, and pull with all my might using my hands on the railing, a push up from under my butt from the physiotherapist, and the weak leg follows. Five instructional steps, one at a time, just to proceed up the first step.

And a new set of instructions for going down the stairs: hang on tight to the railing, the weak leg leads down the first step, strong leg follows. Next step...

"Good job. I'll come back again tomorrow, and we'll go over it again."

Without following those specific instructions, I could not have figured it out myself. I realized the importance of those vital instructions offered to me each time I practiced the stairs. I guess I'm going back to Grandma's house.

20

BACK TO GRANDMA'S HOUSE

"I'M GETTING DISCHARGED BACK TO Grandma's house again. You have to come and stay with me. I have no one to look after me... take time off. Ask your boss. Joy's been here...Neenee was here... I can't do anything myself. Carolyn will be here, but she'll need your help...you'll have to drive me around...you have to come these days...phone me back and let me know right away." I was talking to my sister, Joanne, on the phone. I was adamant, bossy and relentless.

I also texted her; to make sure she understood my urgency. She showed her boss my text and that was all it took for her to receive the time off to come help me.

The staff on the fifteenth floor was excited for me; I was being discharged, again! It was the end of July and the weekend, so Al was there to pack me up and take me away in my wheelchair. I had a sense this discharge was final, and my last day on the fifteenth floor of the Jim Pattison Pavilion. I also believed I was finally on my way to recovery.

As I sat in my wheelchair, Al filled my lap with my belongings, (I could barely see over the top), and draped what was left, over the handles. I was a wide load. Al pushed me and my wheelchair, carefully negotiating, through my hospital room door.

As I exited my room, the hallway seemed extra quiet. Where was everybody? Then as I turned the corner...all the nurses were lined up along the hallway to high five me as I left. What a send-off!

As Al left back for home, my sister, Joanne, arrived for the week. She didn't cook many meals, do laundry or do much of anything around the house, but we sure had a good time. Carolyn had already become my professional, customized, and personal care giver, so I was still well looked after.

Joanne? Well, there was never a dull moment. She drove me around, back and forth to the hospital and all over Vancouver; sometimes, because we were lost.

Our biggest venture out was to Metro Town Shopping Center. I was stressed before we arrived and I wasn't even driving. But I felt it was a big undertaking. Joanne negotiated traffic and attempted to keep with the flow of it across the City, while I unnecessarily, but frantically attempted to assist Carolyn in reading and making sense of the road signs coming at us. The thought of making a wrong turn caused panic in me.

"What did that sign say, Carolyn?"

"What sign...?"

"Oh no, we missed it!" my panic level rising.

"It's OK, Mom. We'll get there..."

There were also the hazards of finding the best underground parking spot for handicaps, getting the wheelchair out of the vehicle in tight quarters, and finding a necessary elevator...

"Why weren't Joanne and Carolyn stressed out like I was?"

Then inside the monstrous mall midst all the crowds; there were groves of people everywhere, bustling about, shopping bags swinging back and forth, everyone going places, turning this way and that, into this shop and that food place. It was a bit hair-raising at first, especially having to rely on the driver's skill negotiating my wheelchair.

It felt good to get back to Grandma's house.

Besides having a lot of fun with Joanne, she was also very encouraging. "You're doing really well, Marge. You look so good. You're getting stronger every day."

I could never hear those words enough.

We had lots of laughs as well; especially Carolyn and I. Joanne told jokes and family stories that kept us bent over in laughter. It was the best exercise for my abdomen and my soul. Her visit was exactly what I needed and I was exhausted every day from it.

I often didn't know from week to week, sometimes even day to day, who would be able to come and look after me. Al came for the weekend and took Carolyn home with him as she was still finishing her clinical at Penticton Regional Hospital.

Each time my sons came to Grandma's house, they became more aware of my vulnerable condition and learned to take care of me. I was beginning to trust them as my sole care giver and towards the end of summer I relied on them to fill in the gaps when there was no one else available.

Levi, my second oldest son, and his girlfriend Danielle took me out in my wheelchair to Stanley Park along the seawall for a day. I appreciated their effort that was required in taking me out.

They knew how to put up with me too. On one of my regular outpatient appointment days, I got myself into a dreadful mood; all worked up about "wasting" my day at the hospital on a day they were out visiting.

"We can come visit you." Levi suggested over the phone from Grandma's house after a few hours of me sulking in my treatment room.

"No, don't come here. It'll be boring for you...I'll be here all day, AGAIN." I continued pouting and grumbling most of the day; staring at and hating the big flower picture on the wall facing me as I lay on the bed. (After looking at that same flower for many months, I especially didn't like it today.)

Even when I returned to Grandma's house I plopped myself on the couch and cried openly, battling with my emotions.

"Let's play cards," Danielle suggested.

That's when I realized and regretted my childish behavior. We could have played cards at the hospital... But instead, I had worked myself up into such a stupor. "Why did I act like that so often? And how did they put up with me?" I wondered momentarily.

"Danielle..." I called from my bed one day; feeling a panic attack coming on. "Please stay with me..." I pleaded as she entered my room.

Without hesitation Danielle came onto my bed and snuggled with me, staying until I calmed down.

Levi made me feel safe and secure. No matter where we were, he was always right there next to me, close, and holding my hand when I needed it. His presence gave me a sense of protection that calmed me.

"How are you doing, Mom...?"

"I'll get that for you...do you need anything?"

My oldest son Jay and his wife Chelsey came to help too. "Let's go to Starbucks." they'd offer; and would make the effort to take me in my wheelchair into Dunbar Village for a treat.

When my hospital day arrived, they would be up early and ready, making sure I had all I needed for the day. Calmly Jay would drive me through Vancouver rush hour, getting me to the hospital for my appointments with plenty of time to spare. Upon entering my room, Chelsey would take charge; gather my clip board, water bottle, vitals machine, and settle me onto my bed.

"Let me do that for you...," she'd offer; taking all my vitals and recording them for me. It was a real treat to have her step in and take over my responsibilities.

After a long day at the hospital Chelsey offered, "Let me paint your toe nails. How about bright pink...?"

I cheered over the improved look of my oversized, swollen feet.

Jay was always checking on me. "Do you need anything...?

"What can I do for you...?

"Let's get out of the house, where can we go..?"

Spanish Banks was close and one of my favorites.

Jay also recognized how much his Uncle Rob and Auntie Violet were doing for me and intentionally thanked them...

Jay brought my youngest son Zach down with him once to take care of me for a couple of days. They took me on an adventurous trip through Stanley Park.

I felt nervous and anxious as they wheeled me through dirt and gravel paths, not sure if they knew how to get out of the woods! My crotchety behavior flared up: I feared for my safety and wellbeing as we continued on the paths through the forest.

I exerted my commander voice as loud as I could, "Quit laughing and having fun.

"What if we're lost? Did you even look at the map?

"This trail is too rough. What if my wheelchair breaks down? One of my wheels could fall off. Then how will you get me out of here?!"

They thought it was funny; I didn't. My social worker called my behavior "survival mode". It was only a while later that I could joke about my crazy worries.

My children all learned how to look after me; in their own unique way, continually preoccupied with my wellbeing. When I was up to it, we did what Zach wanted; played Mario Cart on the Wii. It was fun, a refreshing change in activity, and very exhausting for me too.

Although I was decreasing my prednisone intake and anticipating slow but sure improvements of my wellbeing, I developed new and peculiar symptoms. When breathing normally I made wheezing sounds. I continually had to clear my throat of mucus and my throat sounded hoarse whenever I spoke. I was even having shortness of breath.

Neenee returned to stay with me for a couple of weeks towards the end of summer and noticed the symptoms too. She suggested we read the pamphlet explaining the side effects of the anti-depressant medication that I had been taking.

"That's where all my symptoms are coming from." I discovered, after thoroughly reading through the pamphlet. Other symptoms included memory loss, difficulty focusing…the long list continued. I already struggled with those symptoms long before, from other drugs I was taking as well.

So I weaned myself off the anti-depressants. After all, my circumstances had improved, my dose was low, and I hadn't been on the drug for very long. Besides I hadn't heard from or seen my psychiatrist since.

A couple of weeks later the symptoms went away entirely and I fared well without the medication; a change in the right direction.

I had one last outing with Neenee before she left for home to Kamloops.

"Would you like to go visit Uncle Paul and Auntie Anne?" she asked one day.

"I guess so," I wondered if it would be too much for me. But the more I thought of the idea, the more excited I became. I dressed up for the occasion; dinner at my Aunt and Uncle's. I wore my new fancy, long top with comfortable leggings I bought at Steveston Village with Neenee.

We were flying down the freeway to Surrey or so it felt; my window rolled down and gulping for air as the wind blew in my face, and vehicles racing loudly past, seemingly so close to ours; it was exhilarating and scary. It had been a long time since I'd been on a freeway.

Initially I felt nervous as we entered their home; awkwardly negotiating my walker in an unfamiliar place and feeling outside of my comfort zone. The dining room table setting was much fancier than what I had been used to in a long time. I noticed the hard wood chair that I would be sitting on... Ouch. I imagined the discomfort. I still hadn't any meat on my behind. Uncle Paul brought a cushion from the couch; much better.

I was reminded of how customized Grandma's house had become for me. I always sat on the same big, soft, sofa-like chair in the living room with my plate on a pillow on my lap. I wore a towel like a bib in case I spilled (It seemed like a long ways for my shaky hands to keep the food on my fork all the way from my plate to my mouth; the towel absorbed many drips.) Usually the TV was on.

This was going to be a challenge for me. I wished for my body, emotions, and strength to hold up for the duration of this social outing. Neenee kept a watchful eye on me, escorting me to the bathroom..., always aware of my limitations and vulnerable state.

More relatives arrived for Auntie Anne's scrumptious peach pie.

Shortly after, "Let's get going, Neenee." I was starting to crash; sweating, shaking. I still had to get to and in the vehicle, and home. Going back to Grandma's house and my bed sounded so inviting. The last of my energy was used preparing for bed. Finally, I lay in bed, smiling, and reminiscing on how well the evening played out.

Well, it was time for Neenee to head home; she had a fishing trip to attend to. She had made my life the best it could be in my circumstances. And now who could look after me? As fall was approaching, my options and ideas were running out.

21

JEAN C. BARBER LODGE

EARLIER IN THE SUMMER I had talked to my brother, Rob, about staying at Grandma's house. It had almost been a year since Violet's mother had passed away. I knew Violet had planned to rent Grandma's house out and yet she wanted me to be able to stay there as long as I needed to. Sometimes I wondered when I would ever go home. There was never a word mentioned about it, but Violet and Rob must have wondered sometimes too! I asked Rob if I could stay until the end of August.

"Of course you can," was his reply.

I was relieved to hear that I had until the end of summer. At the time, I figured that I would be going home by then, but when August arrived, it was clear that I was still not well enough.

"Don't worry about where I will stay in September, Violet. Something will come up," I assured her; although I had no idea where I would go.

"I can't think of what to do. Please figure something out for me," another request for God.

There was a cancer lodge about four blocks from the hospital, specifically for housing out of town cancer patients. It had always been an option for me, but I hadn't ever considered it. I imagined it to be depressing; surrounded by cancer patients day in and day out, and food prepared like I had at the hospital. Plus, Violet's offer for me to stay at her mother's house ended my search for an accommodation before I even started looking. But now I had to think differently for September. It was clear that I wouldn't be going home to Penticton yet; Doctor Smith and I had recently decided that Thanksgiving would be a reasonable goal to set; that is, if no other complications came up. As I considered accommodation options for September, none seemed to fit.

Then, I suddenly had a change of mind about the lodge. I became curious and wanted to investigate it further.

Al wasn't able to come down one weekend, so my cousin Annette offered to stay with me. We had always been close friends growing up, but life took us apart from each other for many years. Now it would be just the two of us. I was excited to spend time with her; the best replacement, ever, for Al that weekend. Plus, I had something important to do that she would be happy to help me with.

"Hey, Mare." (I was addressing Annette.) "Could you take me to the Jean C. Barber Cancer Lodge when you come?"

We went over there Saturday afternoon and had a tour to see if it would work for me. I would be sharing a room and bathroom with a roommate. Three meals served everyday were prepared from scratch in their on-site kitchen. (That appealed to me.) There was a variety of activities you could sign up for. I noticed the piano, puzzles, TV rooms and other activity areas as well. And if there was ever a medical emergency, a nurse was on duty twenty-four hours every day.

I immediately visualized myself staying there. It seemed like the right fit and a good transition from having twenty-four seven care to having some responsibilities. Besides, everyone was getting back into their routines for the fall and I couldn't think of anyone available to look after me. I wasn't able to live on my own yet, so this living situation seemed most appropriate for me. The Mason volunteer drivers would pick me up outside the lodge and take me to and from the hospital for all my appointments. When Al came to visit, he could stay at the lodge as well. Often patients went home on weekends so there was always an available room for Al when he arrived.

"I'll need a room for the whole month of September and the first week of October," I told the lodge receptionist.

"Let's see," she replied, looking at her schedule. "I have a room available at the end of August."

"That's perfect." It would give Violet a couple of days to get her place ready for her new renters.

"That's good timing," the receptionist cheered. "Usually, there's a longer wait for a month's stay. I'm glad it will work out for you."

"Me too." What a relief. I relaxed, knowing I had a place arranged until I went home.

Annette was leaving Sunday morning for a family event in Fort Langley. "Why don't you come along, Mare?"

I thought about it..."It might be too much for me...too early in the morning...well...maybe...OK, I'll go."

I'm glad I did. We strolled by and browsed in quaint little shops, stopped for lunch and ice-cream, and walked the path, (me in my wheelchair), along the Fraser River.

The day before I moved to the lodge, my sister-in-law Heather, came and stayed to pack up my belongings. There was much to do and very little I could do myself. Her son William dropped in at just the right time; we loaded him up with the remaining food items from the kitchen.

I was leaving a wonderful accommodation at Grandma's house, full of many memories for me, my family, my caregivers, and friends who stayed for short visits to support me. But I wasn't sad to go. I was ready to move on, another step in the right direction.

When everything was packed, my brother, Rob, came with his truck and moved it all into my new room at the lodge. Once I settled in and looked back at the previous couple of weeks, I realized again how I was continually looked after.

Heather offered to stay for my first meal at my new home. I was glad for her company and support.

"It will be great here," I told her, as we sat across from each other in the dining room. Our first meal was delicious; much better than I was expecting.

Baerg came later that evening to check on me. She wanted to make sure I could negotiate around OK on my own in my new residence. She had me sit on every different sitting spot in the lodge: the sofas, couches, dining room chairs; we didn't miss any one kind.

"Now get up on your own!" Baerg encouraged as I attempted each sitting spot. "You did it. You'll be OK. I wanted to make sure."

I had many new challenges at the lodge, but nothing that was too overwhelming. I had to adjust to a new eating environment, serve up my own beverages, and utilize other help-yourself food stations. If I forgot something it was a major ordeal to get up off my chair and weave my walker through the busy dining room. I learned fast: get everything you need the first time.

I also quickly learned to negotiate my tray on my walker seat, carefully balancing all my food items, especially after it tipped over once. Everything crashed onto the floor and everyone in the dining room heard the disaster and looked up to see me with my mess.

From then on, diners nervously watched my tray for me. "Marge, move your tray over a bit,!" one called out as I gingerly moved along.

I was the only resident using a walker and people graciously accommodated me.

Not having twenty-four seven care like I was used to at Grandma's house helped me to become more independent. I had to get myself to the cafeteria on time for meals, arrange rides to and from the hospital, and look after my medications. I also had to get used to not having the constant company of a care giver with me and the support and security it gave me.

I signed up for activities on days when I wasn't scheduled to go to the hospital. It was a good way to stimulate my mind and helped in my recovery. I attended painting classes, a "look beautiful" workshop, and enjoyed massages that were available to residents.

I played the piano; read music that I played years ago. It was good for my brain, redeveloped fine motor skills in my fingers, and put muscles back into my hands, wrists, and arms. It was relaxing; and encouraging as I saw my piano playing improve with practice.

I also arranged for some counseling sessions; especially to prepare me for when I went home. I was still very vulnerable and weak, both physically and emotionally, and wasn't sure how I would fare.

As the reality of going home drew nearer, I began to feel anxious, imagining the thought of coping. "What if I couldn't meet my family's expectations? Would they remember how vulnerable I still was? I couldn't cook, clean up, or keep order in the household like I used to? I couldn't even walk without my walker. How would I get up and down the stairs to do laundry? The house seemed so big, just getting from one place in the house to another would be a lot of work. I'd be exhausted before I even did anything. And what if...?"

I would get in a tizzy as the list continued in my head.

The counselor helped me set important and realistic goals for myself for when I went home. She gave me practical ideas and tools to help me achieve those goals, and wrote them all down so I could refer to them if needed.

I decided I'd make one of the spare bedrooms at home my quiet place. I could keep the door closed from the daily household action if I needed to rest. I had to remember that my role at home would be very small and my focus had to be to recover. I needed to separate myself from my family's everyday business; I imagined myself becoming overly anxious over affairs that were not in my control. They had coped without me for almost a year and would be able to continue to cope without me. Having my own room would help separate myself when I needed to.

I finally felt the worst of this journey was over. I had conquered the GVHD, my bleeding had stopped, and nothing seemed life threatening anymore. My broken hip was a real setback, but I could work at the exercises I had been given by my physiotherapist, and I had equipment set up for me that could get me around the house.

But another concern was my bone marrow, "Would it ever start producing its own blood cells again? How? And when? Would I have to go to the hospital every other day in Penticton to get blood products?"

"Your body has gone through tremendous trauma in the last year and it is struggling to cope; some of your natural body functions have shut down in its struggle," Doctor Smith had explained. "I don't know how long it will take for your bone marrow to start producing blood cells again..."

I needed another miracle.

It didn't take long; I called it my third miracle. I was ecstatic when my long visits at the hospital suddenly shortened because less blood products were needed! Some days I didn't even need blood! The last two weeks prior to going home I received no blood products at all; my bone marrow was producing its own blood cells.

I looked forward to any opportunities for outings while staying at the lodge. The lodge offered small bus trips on Sunday afternoons to different attractions around the Vancouver area; I always signed up. Plus, offers from friends and relatives; I never turned any down.

My sister-in-law Violet called once. "Are you free this afternoon?"

We drove down to False Creek where she pushed me all around in my wheelchair. It was a beautiful, late summer day and I was reminded of how much I had been able to enjoy the beauty that Vancouver offered. We found an inviting café next to the marina where we stopped for a break and snack.

Almost a year ago, when I first had my transplant, I made a special friend, Mahshid. She also had a transplant similar to me around the same time. However, she struggled from day one of her transplant. I met her while we both walked the halls of our hospital floor. She was very sick and walked very slowly. I was well and went many times around the halls, passing, and meeting up with her several times. I always admired her determination to walk no matter how weak and fragile she was. Her sister, Mojgan, spent a lot of time caring for her and so I became friends with both of them. We kept in touch and met at the hospital when our treatment appointments were on the same days; Sister Mojgan always by Mahshid's side.

While I was staying at the lodge, Mojgan texted me to let me know Mahshid was feeling strong and having a good day. So Mojgan planned a day for us in Vancouver. I was so excited: first, that Mahshid was doing well and second, for the opportunity to go out.

Mojgan picked me up outside the lodge. We drove into North Van, where she took us to an Iranian restaurant for lunch. I was excited to see Mahshid so strong, moving much faster than I was this time, and out of the hospital setting! It was a happy time for us. I assumed during our last visit that Mahshid was finally recovering; like I was.

But she wasn't. Like Mojgan said, "She was having a good day." ... one of few good days. When I was home, Mojgan phoned to tell me that Mahshid had passed away, seventeen months after her transplant.

Al continued to visit me every weekend while I stayed at the lodge. The wheelchair put on many miles during those weekends. It had been an exceptionally dry summer and fall in Vancouver, so weather rarely kept us from being outside for the day. Al would have a quick power nap when he arrived and then we would head out for the rest of the day and evening: trekking across Cambie St. Bridge, going through downtown Vancouver, Gas Town, China Town, back across Burrard St. or Granville St. Bridge, along False Creek, and back up to the lodge at about 9:00 at night. Every so often, I would get out of my wheelchair and push it a short distance. That way I got some exercise; and holding onto the wheelchair gave me the support and stability that I needed. Although my taste buds didn't work, (Doctor Smith said it was a result of the medication and trauma my body suffered from), I still enjoyed stopping for coffee and going out for dinner; trying unique cafés along the way. I loved the City of Vancouver. I felt privileged to have explored much of it first hand in the last year. Plus, viewing Greater Vancouver from the fifteenth floor of the Jim Pattison Pavilion for hours at a time helped orient me when walking outside.

I was also able to enjoy being in public in Vancouver because I was anonymous. Only those close to me in this journey were familiar with my abnormal appearance and situation. (The second looks and stares from passersby, [strangers], didn't bother me.) However, in my hometown of Penticton, I wouldn't be able to easily avoid the risk of bumping into acquaintances or the awkward conversations that could result of it. In Vancouver I wasn't self-conscious about my appearance or circumstances; I felt free to be myself; making every day out in the City a great day.

As tiresome as it was, Al loved coming to Vancouver too. He looked forward to getting out of Penticton, and now, finally, watching my health improve each time he came made it much less burdensome. My Thanksgiving goal of going home was coming to a reality.

It cost me about $55.00 per day to stay at the lodge. It included three meals and a bathroom cleaning each day. Once a week the room was vacuumed, and the bed and bathroom linens were changed.

Although the cost to stay there was very reasonable, it was another expense on top of many other costs incurred during my illness. We were expected to settle our bill every Friday. I assumed that they kept my credit card number on file because every time I went to square up for the week, the receptionist would tell me that they had already put the payment through. I was a bit baffled though; my roommate had to go in person every Friday to put her payment transaction through. And Al noticed that none of the weekly transactions showed up on our credit card statement. So when I went to the office to pay up before I left, I prepared myself for a big bill.

"Your bill has already been paid," she said, brushing me off, smirking, and looking away.

"What do you mean? Every time I come to pay my bill you tell me it's already been paid. There aren't any transactions on our credit card statements either; I don't think we've paid anything..." I was confused.

"Well," she started, smiling at me. "She didn't want you to know."

"Know what...who?" I didn't understand.

"...the lady who has been paying your bill every week."

"What? Who is it? You have to tell me...! Is it Anne...?"

It was Anne; and her husband John. Along with them, there were others who gave of their finances to help pay for the many expenses that we incurred while going through this journey. Once when I went in for my treatment at the hospital, I found a card on my clip board with a check inside. My aunt and uncle, cousin, and family members; many supported us with their finances.

22

GOING HOME AGAIN

THE THOUGHT OF GOING HOME this time felt a lot different than when I went home last Christmas. I had mixed emotions; sometimes feeling scared and vulnerable, other times feeling excited and impatient. Sometimes it was hard for me to believe going home was really going to happen. I had to work at keeping my emotions under control. Sometimes Ativan helped to calm me down.

I had been in Vancouver for six months. I had come a long way since my final discharge from the hospital, but I had an even longer way to go in my recovery when I got home.

A few days before Thanksgiving weekend, my oldest son Jay came to pick me up. There wasn't much to pack up; Al had already started taking things home with him on weekends. Al, Zach, and Jay's wife Chelsey were home to welcome me. I went to our couch in the living room. Chelsey added a couple of pillows around me for comfort, immediately noticing my frailty. I appreciated that. Sitting on my couch now felt a lot different than before. My body was fragile and needed lots of support.

But, it was good to be home.

That night I slept in Carolyn's room, as I had planned. It felt good; a restful place for me. I remembered the goals I had made for myself with my counselor in Vancouver. It was important to focus on my recovery.

The following day was quiet. Carolyn and Levi were away at university, Zach at school, and Al at work. Alone now, I walked around the main floor with my walker, (I wasn't ready to take the stairs down just yet).

Inside my house, it felt so still, almost like the house had been deserted. (I had been away a long time.) And yet, as I peered into each room, everything looked the same, as if I had never left...except that it all needed a good cleaning.

I sat in the living room looking around. Our large windows facing the backyard were filthy. They hadn't been cleaned since the last time I was home. There were unpacked boxes everywhere, mostly mine, that had come home the last few trips with Al. There were book keeping baskets and boxes of papers strewn all over that needed to be filed. Even the mess from our renovations was just as I had left it; paint cans, rollers and brushes, trays, and newspaper still on the floor in the dining area.

"Why didn't they clean up before I got home?" I wondered. "It's a disaster in here. They had it spic and span when I had come home at Christmas. How will I ever get through all this stuff?"

But then I remembered. It had been a long haul for them too. Carolyn and Levi weren't home to help out. Al and Zach had been on their own, flying by the seat of their pants. I decided the mess was a compliment. I was missed...a lot.

Al and Zach moved all the boxes and mess out of the living room into the spare room. I closed the door. Now I wouldn't get stressed out looking at it every day, knowing that I couldn't clean any of it up myself. When I was ready, and I didn't know how long that would be, I would go into the spare room and sort through the mess, one box at a time.

My world would be very small for a while; me in my house. There were so many things I couldn't do. But I had to focus on the things I could do: make Zach's lunch for school, make my bed, do a few dishes, and look after myself.

No one had expectations on me. They just went about their business, leaving me to rest. I guess they were used to not having me around. But they did keep telling me how much better it was to have me home and how important I was to the family.

My neighbor Karen came to say hi. She picked up the broom and swept the floor. Then she left and came back with a mop; and washed my floors. "If you need anything, ever, let me know...I'll be here."

Thanksgiving weekend came. It was good to be home, but I struggled with how different it was. I had always been in charge of preparing our traditional turkey dinner with all the dressings, adding leaves and chairs to extend the dining table to accommodate extra family, and setting my fancy china, silverware, napkins, and odds and ends of crystal wine goblets on the table. In general; bossing everyone around.

But not this year; I didn't help with any of the preparations. Everyone else pitched in. I sat on the couch, frail, feeling useless, and holding back tears. I was reminded of the difficult journey I had trod, still raw in my heart. Would I ever be what I used to be?

There was a quiet knock on the door. My kids greeted my parents at the door before I could even lift myself off the couch to welcome them. As I watched them enter the living room, I was reminded how my body was slower, older, and weaker than theirs. After dinner, while we visited in the living room, slowly and quietly, and with the support of my walker, I left the room; hearing my slippers slowly shuffling small steps along the hardwood floor...and tears falling. I was the only one that needed to lie down and rest.

But I was doing the right thing; taking care of myself; leaving when I needed rest and quiet; doing what I was supposed to.

After the weekend everyone went back home to their routines again. I started having my own; bed exercises every morning, then a shower, a simple breakfast, and a nap. Every week I gradually accomplished more household tasks and lay down less during the day. I did more dishes and they felt lighter as my muscles grew stronger. I began cooking and went up and down the stairs to do laundry.

Improvements continued in many ways. My skin cleared up; the purple blotches disappeared. My blood sugar readings improved; no more diabetes or poking myself to check my blood sugar. My upper body slimmed down. The puffiness in my face and neck gradually left. Although my hair had grown back in, I kept losing much of it; but now, it stopped falling out, started growing longer, and got thicker. My voice gained strength. My eye sight improved, (now I only needed my eye glasses for reading again), and the achy pressure behind them gradually went away. When I worked in my kitchen I stood more, instead of sitting on my walker seat. I slept better, longer intervals, and sometimes right through the night, even without Ativan or sleeping pills. My energy level increased.

My right leg gained strength, although my left leg fell behind. I was told the healing may take much longer than usual because of all the complications I had when I broke my left hip. But that helped me to be patient.

Al took me for many wheelchair walks along the lakes bordering Penticton. Gradually, when I stepped out of my wheelchair, I pushed it more often and for longer distances. A couple of months later, I retired the wheelchair and used my walker instead. My walking distances continually increased. Then I graduated to walking poles. Now I occasionally use a cane, but hoping to toss that for good one day too.

By Christmas I was completely off my prednisone medication. Other medications were tapered down with no signs of recurring GVHD. After a few months, my blood levels were in the normal zone.

My emotions gradually stabilized. I cried less often and sometimes was able to talk about my journey without all the tears that often accompanied it. When I struggled with my emotions, I'd remind myself, "That was then, but you're not there anymore. Move on and live in the present; one day at a time."

On and on...the constant changes and improvements that I noticed in my body motivated me to keep working at it. I am still recovering, but I can see how far I have come; pictures, my journal, and now my story remind me.

After Christmas I mentioned to some friends, "What can I do in the evenings? I'm so bored; tired of TV...I've tried a few other activities as well but can't find anything that interests me. Every day by dinner time my body is so tired and sore, but my mind isn't. Any ideas?"

"If you write your story, I'll read it." Linda, one of my friends, suggested.

Initially I wasn't interested. But then, one evening in January, I got my lap top out and started writing my story. I was hooked. I found it relaxing, stimulating for my mind, therapeutic, and very engaging. (After all, it was about me.)

It quickly became my winter evening routine. I kept everything I needed on my living room couch: lap top, pillow, throw, eye glasses, and journal. After dinner I'd make myself a cup of tea and settle into my spot; putting my weak leg up to rest. Comfortable, resting, and engaged, under the warm light of my lamp, I typed my story; no rush, no pressure. I felt privileged. I was given the opportunity with the gifts of much time, desire, and ability to write.

I hope you enjoyed reading my story as much as I enjoyed writing it.

Recent photo

Notes

All Holy Bible scripture quotes are taken
from the New International Version

1. Isaiah 41:10
2. John 15:7,8
3. Ecclesiastes 3:1,2
4. Isaiah 55:9

CPSIA information can be obtained
at www.ICGtesting.com
Printed in the USA
BVHW081321221220
596013BV00001B/53